Ethernet Networking Clearly Explained

R

Ethernet Networking Clearly Explained

Jan L. Harrington

**Morgan
Kaufmann**

AN IMPRINT OF ACADEMIC PRESS

San Diego   San Francisco   New York   Boston
London   Sydney   Tokyo

Riverside Community College
Library
4800 Magnolia Avenue
Riverside, CA 92506

TK 5105.8 .E83 H37 1999

Harrington, Jan L.

Ethernet networking clearly
  explained

This book is printed on acid-free paper.

Copyright © 1999 by Academic Press

All rights reserved.
No part of this publication may be reproduced or transmitted in any form or by any means, electronic
or mechanical, including photocopy, recording, or any information storage and retrieval system,
without permission in writing from the publisher.

All brand names and product names mentioned in this book are trademarks or registered trademarks
of their respective companies.

ACADEMIC PRESS
A division of Harcourt Brace & Company
525 B Street, Suite 1900, San Diego, CA 92101-4495, USA
http://www..academicpress.com

Academic Press
24–28 Oval Road, London NW1 7DX, United Kingdom
http://www.hbuk.co.uk/ap/

Morgan Kaufmann
340 Pine Street, Sixth Floor, San Francisco, CA 94104-3205
http://www.mkp.com

Library of Congress Catalog Card Number: 99-60976
International Standard Book Number: 0-12-326427-8

Printed in the United States of America
99 00 01 02 03 IP 9 8 7 6 5 4 3 2 1

Contents

Chapter 5: Connecting Network Segments   **63**

Chapter 6: Integrating Wireless Transmissions   **99**

Part Three: Equipping an Ethernet with Hardware and Software

Part Four: Ethernet Solution Examples

Preface

Computer networks—interconnected collections of computing hardware and software—are an unavoidable characteristic of the current computing environment. You might use a network to connect to a printer located in another room, to interact with the Internet, or to share files with another user in your company who is working in another city. Each of these types of networks has its own hardware and software requirements, all of which is surrounded by a bewildering array of terminology.

In this book you will be reading about one particular kind of networking—Ethernet—that is used primarily by networks that are contained within a single physical location. (Remote users can access the network through telecommunications lines, but the permanent parts of the network are typically located in one building or a group of buildings located in close physical proximity.)

If you need to design, install, and manage a network in such an environment, then this book will give you an in-depth understanding of the technology involved in an Ethernet network.

Probably the toughest part of understanding networks is the jargon. If you're unfamiliar with networking terminology and acronyms, then a sentence like "To hook up to 10BASE2, you connect the BNC connector to the NIC" is meaningless gibberish. One of the major goals of this book is therefore to demystify the secret language of networks for you, so that you can speak in acronyms just like the rest of the network gurus.

One of my greatest frustrations with networking books is that they often focus on only one layer of the network. To be techically accurate, "Ethernet" only refers to one part of the hardware. However, if you are going to be responsible for an Ethernet network, then you need to know a lot more than just how to choose and configure your network hardware. You also need information about the types of devices you can attach to your network and what types of software you will need to make it all work. In addition, you will probably want to give some thought to managing the network. This book therefore goes beyond the hardware aspects of Ethernet to look at the entire network from bottom to top.

Another major concern with writing a book of this type is the level of technical detail. How much do you really need or want to know about how network signals are transmitted? If you want to know which specific signals are carried on which wires within a network cable, then this is not the book for you. However, if you want enough technical detail to be able to make intelligent choices about what types of transmission media you will use for your network and the way in which you interconnect the parts of that network, then you are holding the right volume.

What You Need to Know

To understand the material in this book, you should have a thorough knowledge of basic PC hardware and at least one PC operating system (for example, Windows 95, some flavor of UNIX, or the Macintosh OS). You should also be comfortable with basic PC software such as word processors, e-mail, and World Wide Web browsers.

Acknowledgments

Writing a book for Morgan Kaufmann is an absolute delight. I'd like to thank both Ken Morton, my editor, and Gabrielle Billeter, his assistant, for all their help. And of course, much thanks to the production editor, Julio Esperas, and Bryna Fischer, a copy editor with a very fine eye for detail. And finally, let us not forget the wonderful technical illustrator, James A. Houston of Visual Graphics, Inc., and the extremely knowledgeable technical editor, Mike Avery.

In addition, a large number of vendors gave us permission to use illustrations and photos of their products. My thanks go out to all of them. (You can find contact information for those vendors in Appendix B.)

Finally, thanks once again to my agent, Carole McClendon, for putting me in touch with this publisher.

JLH

http://www.blackgryphonltd.com

Part One

Introduction

The first two chapters of this book present some introductory conceptual material about networking and Ethernet. By the time you finish reading them, you will understand exactly what Ethernet is and the part it plays in your overall network.

1

Introduction

One of the biggest problems when discussing networking is knowing where to start. The subject of computer networks is one of those areas for which you have to "know everything to do anything." Therefore, to ease you into the process, this chapter begins with some basic networking terminology and then looks at exactly what it means when we use the word *Ethernet*.

The Anatomy of a Network

A computer *network* is a combination of hardware and software that allows computers and other peripherals (for example, printers and modems) to communicate with one another through some form of telecommunications media (for example, telephone lines).

3

> *Note: As you read material about data communications, you may see references to POTS lines. POTS stands for "plain old telephone service."*

Networks can be classified by the distances they cover and whether they include web technology:

- *LAN* (local area network): A network confined to a small geographic area—such as a floor, single building, or group of buildings in close physical proximity (for example, a college campus or an office park)—that is almost always owned by a single organization. The organization owns the telecommunications lines as well as the hardware connected to the network. LAN today typically refers to a network that does not include a World Wide Web server.
- *Intranet*: A LAN that includes a World Wide Web server.
- *MAN* (metropolitan area network): An outdated term describing a network that covers an entire city. Today, the concept of a MAN has been replaced largely by the WAN.
- *WAN* (wide area network): A network that covers a large geographic area, such as a city, state, or one or more countries. Although a WAN may be owned by a single organization, the network usually includes telecommunications media (for example, telephone lines or satellite transmissions) that are leased from telecommunications providers.
- *Internet*: When in all lowercase letters (*internet*), a WAN that connects multiple LANs into a larger network. When written with a leading uppercase letter (*Internet*), it is the global network that supports the World Wide Web. Because of the potential for confusion between internet and Internet, the term *internet* is rarely used today.

The technologies we will be discussing in this book are applicable primarily to LANs and intranets. Although we will be discussing connecting LANs to the Internet, the focus is on creating and maintaining networks that serve small to medium-size workgroups.

Parts of a Network

A computer network is made up of three major components:

- *Hardware*: The equipment that connects to the network. Typically, this includes computers, printers, and modems. Each distinct piece of hardware on a network is known as a *node*. In addition to the hardware that actually uses the network to transfer data to perform work for an organization, a network may contain specialty hardware that helps manage the network and connect it to other networks. Such hardware includes routers, bridges, switches, hubs, repeaters, and gateways. You will read about network hardware of these types throughout this book.

  Each device on a network is identified by two types of addresses. The first is a hardware address that physically identifies the piece of equipment. In many cases, this address is set by the hardware manufacturer and is not easily changed. These addresses, known as *MAC* (*media access control*) addresses, must be unique throughout the entire network. If a manufacturer happens to produce hardware with duplicated MAC addresses, then the network that uses that hardware cannot function.

  The second type of address is a software address that is added by the software that handles data transmission. The software address can be changed as needed.

- *Software*: The programs that manage the transfer of data throughout the network, most commonly known as *network operating systems*.

- *Transmission media*: The cables or wireless signals that carry data from one node to another.

In addition, there must be interfaces between the hardware and the network. These often take the form of expansion boards that are added to pieces of hardware (*network interface cards*, or NICs, such as that in Figure 1-1), although a significant number of today's computers and printers are shipped with network hardware already installed on their motherboards. Depending on the type of transmissions media in use, a network may also need hardware connections between the media coming from a piece of hardware and the network itself.

Figure 1-1:   A network interface card (NIC) (courtesy of Farallon Corp.)

In Figure 1-2 you can see a generalized diagram of how the hardware fits together. Each device you want to connect to a network must have either a network interface card or networking hardware installed on its motherboard. The NIC (or the motherboard) contains a port to which a cable can be attached. That cable runs to the network, tapping into the network transmission medium with some sort of attachment unit.

There is a bewildering variety of hardware and transmission media available for LANs and intranets. We will therefore be spending a considerable amount of time in this book looking at hardware choices.

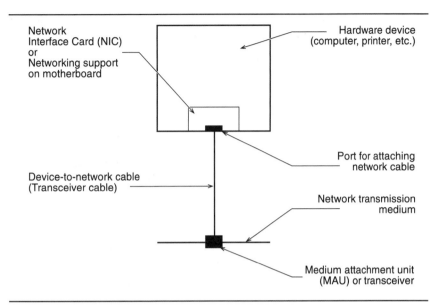

Figure 1-2:   Generalized network connections

Data Communications Protocols

The software used to transfer messages over a network are known as network *protocols*, specifications of how a computer will format and transfer data. If a computer contains implementations of a set of protocols, theoretically it can communicate with any other computer that has implementations of the same protocols. The protocols provide a standardized way for computers to format and transmit data to one another. Protocols ensure, if you will, that computers communicating over data communications lines will be speaking the same language.

There are many standard sets of protocols in use. However, those that you are most likely to use with Ethernet include:

♦ *TCP/IP* (Transmission Control Protocol/Internet Protocol): The protocols used by the Internet. Because of the influence of the Internet, TCP/IP has been the most widely used group of protocols in the world. There are

implementations of TCP/IP for virtually every computing platform today.

*Note: TCP/IP actually originated with the UNIX operating
system. It was selected for use by ARPANET, the precursor of
the Internet and had a relatively minor role in networking until
the Internet became widely used in the early 1990s.*

♦ *NetBEUI* (network BIOS extended user interface): The
  protocols used by Windows 95, 98, and NT. NetBEUI was
  originally developed by IBM for OS/2 and was also used
  in Windows for Workgroups.
♦ *IPX/SPX*: The protocols developed for Novell NetWare, a
  network operating system, based on prior work by Xerox
  at its PARC (Palo Alto Research Center) facility. Prior to
  the development of IPX/SPX, TCP/IP was the most
  widely used set of protocols. TCP/IP regained its domi-
  nance with the rise in popularity of the Internet.
♦ *AppleTalk*: A set of protocols designed primarily for use
  by Macintosh computers. However, AppleTalk protocols
  are also available for Windows 95, Windows NT, and
  Linux. They are typically used in networks that are predominantly Macintosh and need to integrate a few Windows machines. AppleTalk forms the foundation for
  AppleShare, Apple Computer's software that manages
  shared files over an AppleTalk network.

It is possible for the same computer to use more than one protocol
stack at the same time. For example, you might be using TCP/IP to
pick up e-mail using a modem and telephone line. At the same time,
your computer could be using AppleTalk to print a file and one of
Novell NetWare's protocols to exchange files with another computer over a LAN.

Each data communications conversation in which your computer
participates uses only one protocol stack. However, because most of
today's operating systems support some form of multitasking, a
computer can handle multiple communications sessions at the
same time, each of which may be using a different set of protocols.

Network Layers

The interaction of network hardware and software can be viewed as being in a layered stack. Each of the three sets of protocols mentioned in the previous section has its own distinct stack.

The TCP/IP Protocol Stack

In Figure 1-3 you will find the TCP/IP stack. Such layering—most commonly known as a *protocol stack*—always has a hardware layer (the *Physical layer* in Figure 1-3) at the bottom. The remaining layers are software and correspond to groups of data communications protocols.

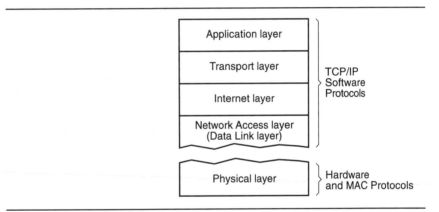

Figure 1-3:   The TCP/IP protocol stack

From the bottom up, the TCP/IP layers are

- ◆ *Network Access layer* (also known as the *Data Link layer*): The protocols in this layer cover the way in which hardware gains access to the transmission media.
- ◆ *Internet layer*: The Internet layer contains protocols that are used when messages must travel between two interconnected LANs or intranets. This is where the protocols for the IP portion of TCP/IP can be found.
- ◆ *Transport layer*: The Transport layer ensure reliable transfer of data, independent of the application programs that

are using the data. This layer contains the TCP portion of
TCP/IP.

♦ *Application layer*: The protocols in this layer are those
found in the programs that a node uses to access the network.

When you obtain networking software, you are getting implementations of protocols at one or more layers in a protocol stack.

The OSI Protocol Stack

The AppleTalk protocol stack and Novell NetWare's protocols are
based on an international standard known as the *OSI* (Open Systems
Interconnect) Reference Model. Adopted by the *ISO* (International
Standards Organization), most network professionals believed that
this standard would become the model for all network protocols.
However, they did not count on the rise of the Internet, which has
made TCP/IP and its protocol stack the basis for most of today's networking. The OSI protocol stack is therefore a theoretical model that
provides a convenient framework for discussing groups of protocols.
Most of today's protocol stacks can be mapped to the OSI layers.

As you can see in Figure 1-4, there is a Physical layer that includes
the hardware that is separate from the software layers above. The
bottom three software layers are relatively equivalent to the bottom
three layers of the TCP/IP protocol stack. However, the Session layer takes over some of the responsibility of managing communication sessions. The Presentation layer acts as an interface between
the Application layer, which as in TCP/IP consists of the user's software, and the Session layer.

A Final Word on Protocol Stacks

The beauty of the layered approach is that hardware and software
can be relatively independent. The software portions of the two
protocol stacks you have seen (TCP/IP and OSI) are independent of
the hardware on which they may be running. For example, TCP/IP
can be used on all types of Ethernet hardware as well as on Token

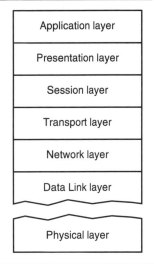

| Application layer |
| Presentation layer |
| Session layer |
| Transport layer |
| Network layer |
| Data Link layer |
| Physical layer |

Figure 1-4:   The ISO Reference Model protocol stack

Ring hardware. AppleTalk, based on the OSI stack, can run on Ethernet and Token Ring hardware, but also on proprietary hardware known as LocalTalk or PhoneNet. IPX/SPX, also, is independent of the hardware on which it is running.

Note: There is some confusion about the terms AppleTalk *and* LocalTalk. *When AppleTalk networking first appeared in 1987, both the protocol stack and the cabling on which it ran were known as AppleTalk. However, Apple became aware that the protocols could run over other types of cabling, so they renamed the cabling LocalTalk. Little new LocalTalk cabling is being installed. Ethernet is just as cheap, today's Macintoshes come with Ethernet built in, and Ethernet is much faster (a minimum of 10 Mbps versus 256 Kbps).*

Network Operating Systems

Although we will discuss network operating systems in some depth in Chapter 8, at this point you should at least be familiar with the names of the software that manages file usage on a network. Those that you are likely to encounter include:

- *Novell NetWare:* Novell NetWare was one of the first network operating systems. It made possible the networking of computers running MS-DOS. NetWare uses DOS to boot the server and then installs itself as an alternative operating system. Although today Novell NetWare can use TCP/IP, its original file transfer protocol was IPX. Novell NetWare requires a server runing the server software and client software on all machines. Novell client software is included in recent Windows releases but must be purchased separately for operating systems such as UNIX, Macintosh OS, and OS/2.
- *Microsoft Windows LAN Manager*: This network operating system is part of Windows for Workgroups, Windows 95, Windows 98, and Windows NT. Network administrators can choose between TCP/IP, IPX/SPX, and NetBEUI as the primary protocol stack.
- *UNIX*: The many variations of the UNIX operating system incorporate TCP/IP as their networking foundation.
- *AppleShare*: AppleShare is an add-on to the Macintosh Operating System that permits the sharing of files from a centralized location. It uses the AppleTalk Filing Protocol running on top of the AppleTalk protocol stack.
- *OS/2 LAN Server*: OS/2 is a network-ready operating system and can work with TCP/IP, IPX/SPX, or NetBEUI. However, currently OS/2 is less widely used than most other operating systems.
- *World Wide Web*: Although you may not think of a web browser as networking software, a web browser shares files using the HTTP protocol from the TCP/IP protocol stack. It is therefore a reasonable alternative to look to Internet protocols to manage file sharing on an Ethernet.

What Ethernet Really Means

Where does Ethernet fit into all of this? In the Physical layer. In a LAN or intranet, there are many pieces of hardware trying to gain access to the network transmission media at the same time. However, a network cable or wireless transmission frequency can physically only allow one node to use it at any given moment. There must therefore be some way to control which node has control of the medium (a *media access control*, or MAC, protocol).

Ethernet is a MAC protocol. It is one way to regulate physical access to network transmission media. You will learn exactly how it works in Chapter 2.

> *Note: At the time this book was written, the major alternative to Ethernet was Token Ring. However, in a survey taken by Computerworld in early 1998, more than 60 percent of Token Ring users said they were migrating toward Ethernet. Ethernet is much cheaper than Token Ring and has also become much faster. Just as TCP/IP has beaten out the OSI protocol stack to become the most widely used group of network protocols, Ethernet would seem to be pushing Token Ring out of the running.*

Types of Ethernet

Today there are actually three flavors of Ethernet, distinguished by their transmission speeds:

- ◆ *Standard Ethernet*: Transfers data at a maximum of 10 megabits per second (abbreviated as 10M bps). At today's prices, it is possible to set up a simple eight-node standard Ethernet LAN for less than $300. This assumes that all of the nodes require expansion boards. However, many of today's computers and printers ship with standard Ethernet support built into their motherboards. If all of the nodes already have Ethernet support, then the cost to set up the same eight-node network would be less

than $100. For a very small workgroup with limited net-
working needs (for example, printer sharing and a little
bit of file sharing), standard Ethernet is a very economi-
cal networking solution.

♦ *Fast Ethernet*: Transfers data at a maximum of 100 Mbps.
At the time this book was written costs were two to three
times that of standard Ethernet but decreasing rapidly.

♦ *Gigabit Ethernet*: Transfers data at a maximum of 1 gigabit
per second (abbreviated as 1 Gbps). At the time this book
was written, Gigabit Ethernet hardware was just becoming widely available. As the newest technology in the
Ethernet family, it is still relatively expensive. However,
as Gigabit Ethernet becomes more pervasive, the prices
of Fast Ethernet will drop significantly and perhaps
within a year approach the levels where standard Ethernet prices are currently. Therefore, although Gigabit
Ethernet is practical only for larger networks at this time,
its presence in the marketplace may push down Fast
Ethernet prices to the point where Fast Ethernet completely supplants standard Ethernet. The logical conclu-
sion to this process is that eventually, Gigabit Ethernet
will also become cheap enough for the desktop.

When considering Ethernet speeds, keep in mind that the transfer
rates associated with each type of Ethernet are maximums. In practice, it is rare to achieve the highest transfer rate. Many factors limit
network speed, including the nature of the transmission media, the
amount of traffic on the network, and the speeds of the hardware
manipulating the network. In addition, an Ethernet that supports
between 30 and 60 percent utilization is considered to be saturated.
You will therefore never realize total use of your network media.

Given that Ethernet and the data transmission protocols that run on
top of it (TCP/IP, IPX/SPX, and AppleTalk) are independent, when
you choose Ethernet over some other form of physical network, you
are restricting your hardware choices rather than your software
choices. As you will see, the type of Ethernet you choose (as well as
your choice of Ethernet rather than Token Ring, ARCNet, FDDI,

CDDI, or ATM), dictates to some extent what hardware you use. However, your software choices are not limited.

The Speed and Bandwidth Connection

The three types of Ethernet are defined in terms of their maximum transmission speeds. Nonetheless, they can in most cases use the same type of wiring. Assume, for example, that standard, Fast, and Gigabit Ethernet are all using the same wire medium. Electrical signal can travel at only one physical speed over the medium. How can this be true if there are three Ethernet speeds?

The answer lies in how we actually look at speed. The measures of Ethernet speed are actually what is known as *throughput*, the number of bits that arrive at a destination per unit time. There are two ways to affect throughput. The first is to speed up the rate at which the bits travel, but this is dictated by the physical properties of the wire. Since we cannot speed up the travel rate of a single bit, the only other choice is to increase the number of bits traveling together. For example, if you can send four bits per unit time, your throughput will be greater than if you can send only one. This is directly analogous to widening a road from two to four lanes but leaving the maximum speed limit the same. Widening the road does not allow an individual car to travel faster, but does allow more cars to cover the same distance in the same period of time.

The number of bits that can travel together at the same time represents the *bandwidth* of the transmission medium. If we can increase the bandwidth, we can increase the throughput without changing the maximum physical transfer speed of bits down the wire. Fiber optic cabling, for example, is very fast not only because each bit can travel at the speed of light, but because so many tiny glass fibers can be bound together into a single cable to provide a high bandwidth.

Ethernet Standards

The types of Ethernet about which you have just read are defined in a set of standards prepared by the Institute of Electrical and Electronic Engineers (IEEE). The committee in charge of the standards for LANs is known as IEEE LAN 802, and the group within it that handles media access controls standards as 802.3. Each 802.3 standard describes a method for media access control and the transmission media that should be supported.

> *Note: Although the name of the IEEE may not suggest that the organization has anything to do with computing, keep in mind that the IEEE predates computers. It has evolved over time to encompass a wide range of computing standards and applications.*

Although in most cases you won't be concerned directly with the specifications themselves and the rather strange numbering scheme that goes along with them, you may find that equipment and cable vendors use the standard numbers to identify the type of Ethernet for which a product is appropriate. You should therefore at least be familiar with which type of Ethernet each standard represents. This book therefore will identify the standards that accompany each type of Ethernet cabling as we explore hardware details in the following chapters.

A Bit of Ethernet History

Originally, Ethernet was the brainchild of one person: Robert Metcalfe. In the early 1970s, while working at Xerox PARC on the "office of the future" project, Metcalfe was intrigued by a radio network in Hawaii known as AlohaNet. One of the problems faced by AlohaNet's media access control was that its maximum effeciency was 17 percent: That is, a maximum of 17 percent of the transmission units sent actually reached their destination. According to Metcalfe, the unreceived portions of the transmissions were "lost in the ether."

Metcalfe developed an alternative media access control method that allowed up to 90 percent of the transmission units to reach their destination. Originally known as "experimental Ethernet," it transferred up to 3 Mbps. As you can see in Metcalfe's original drawing in Figure 1-5, he refers to the cabling along with data travel as "the ether," hence the name *Ethernet*.

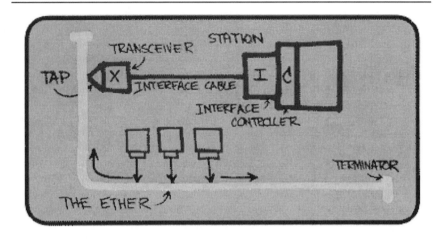

Figure 1-5:   Bob Metcalfe's original drawing for Ethernet (courtesy of Bob Metcalfe)

> *Note: Bob Metcalfe went on to found the 3Com Corporation and currently is a networking pundit and guru. His columns appear in InfoWorld and elsewhere.*

The first Ethernet specifications were published in 1980 by a consortium of commercial hardware vendors—Digital Equipment Corporation (now a part of Compaq Corp.), Intel, and Xerox (DIX). By that time, the transmission speed had been increased to 10 Mbps.

The IEEE adopted Ethernet as a LAN standard and published its initial specifications in 1985. Later, Ethernet was also endorsed as a standard by the ISO. Ethernet is therefore an international standard for one way in which nodes on a LAN can gain access to transmission media.

2

How Ethernet Works

Regardless of the type of Ethernet you choose, the basic way in which data are packaged to travel over the network and the way in which devices gain access to the network media remain the same. In this chapter we will therefore look at both the packaging of the data and the way that Ethernet provides media access control.

Ethernet Frames

To transmit a message across an Ethernet, a device constructs an Ethernet *frame,* a package of data and control information that travels as a unit across the network. A small message may fit in a single frame, but large messages are split between multiple frames.

Note: Because software protocol stacks like TCP/IP refer to their units of transmission as "packets," Ethernet frames are also often called packets.

There are two general types of frames. The first carries meaningful data (the content of messages two devices want to exchange). The second carries network management information. Nonetheless, the general structure of both types of frames is identical.

An Ethernet frame varies in size from 64 bytes to 1529 bytes. It is made up of the nine fields that you can see in Figure 2-1.

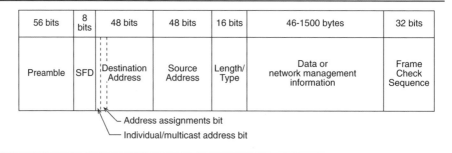

Figure 2-1:   An Ethernet frame (IEEE 802.3 standard)

- *Preamble*: The preamble contains a group of 64 bits that are used to help the hardware synchronize itself with the data on the network. If a few bits of the preamble are lost during transmission, no harm occurs to the message itself. The preamble therefore also acts as a buffer for the remainder of the frame.

  The last 8 bits of the preamble are used as a *start frame delimiter*. This marks the end of the preamble and the start of the information-bearing parts of the frame.

- *Destination address*: The destination address (48 bits) contains the physical address of the device that is to receive the frame.

  The first two bits of this field have special meaning. If the first bit is 0, then the address represents a hardware address of a single device on the network. However, if the first bit is 1, then the address is what is known as a *multicast address* and the frame is addressed to a group of devices. The second bit indicates where physical device addresses have been set. If the value is 0, then addresses have been set by the hardware manufacturer (global addressing). When addresses are set by those maintaining the network, the value is 1 (local addressing).

Note: A device's physical address is distinct from its software address, such as the addresses used by TCP/IP. (For example, the author's printer has a TCP/IP address of 205.1.1.5 and an Ethernet address of 00:C0:B0:02:15:75.) One of the jobs of data communications protocols is therefore to translate between hardware and software addresses. TCP/IP, for example, uses Address Resolution Protocol (ARP) to map TCP/IP addresses onto Ethernet addresses.

- *Source address*: The 48 bits of the source address field contain the hardware address of the device sending the frame.
- *Length field*: The contents of the length field depends on the type of frame. If the frame is carrying data, then the length field indicates how many bytes of meaningful data are present. However, if the frame is carrying management information, then the length field indicates the type of management information present in the frame.
- *Data field*: The data field carries a minimum of 46 bytes and a maximum of 1500 bytes. If there are less than 46 bytes of data, the field will be padded to the minimum length.
- *Frame check sequence* (FCS): The last field (also known as a *cyclical redundancy check*, or CRC, field) contains 32 bits used for error checking. The bits in this field are set by the transmitting device based on the pattern of bits in the data field. The receiving device then regenerates the FCS. If what the receiving device obtains does not match what is in the frame, then some bits were changed during transmission and some type of transmission error has occurred.

Note: FCS error checking will not catch all errors, but it is certainly more effective than having no error checking at all!

Ethernet Media Access

Whenever a device connected to an Ethernet network wants to send a message, it places that message in one or more frames. However, only one frame can be transmitted on any given network segment at a time because the network itself—at least conceptually—is a single electrical pathway that can carry only one signal at a time. A device must therefore take control of the network, making sure that it is not in use by another device, before it begins sending a frame. This is what media access control is all about.

To understand how Ethernet's MAC protocol works, you must first know something about how an Ethernet network is laid out (its *topology*). At the most fundamental level, all Ethernet networks use a *bus topology*, a layout in which the devices all connect to a single network transmission line. As you can see in Figure 2-2, the ends of the bus are unconnected. Each devices simply taps into the bus, which is conceptually—although not necessarily physically—a single unbroken transmission pathway. (You will see later in this chapter that there are alternative ways of connecting devices to an Ethernet that make it appear as if the topology is something other than a bus. However, when you look inside the network connections, it is still the simple bus.)

Note: There doesn't seem to be any well-accepted story about why an electronic pathway into which devices plug is called a bus. However, think of the bus as a vehicle that bits ride from one place to the other. That is as good an explanation as any!

To send a frame, a device makes sure that the bus is not in use and then transmits its frame. All other devices on the network read each frame as it passes. If the address is for another device, the device reading the frame ignores the rest of the frame. However, when a

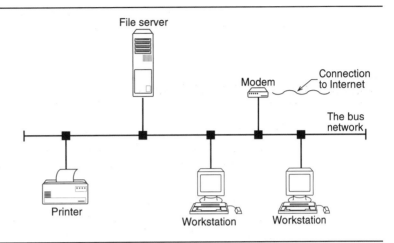

Figure 2-2:   A simple bus topology for an Ethernet network

device recognizes its own address in the frame, it then continues to handle the rest of the frame.

The trick in this scheme is to make sure the bus is not in use. Ethernet hardware is designed to detect the presence of a frame on the network. When this condition occurs, a device detects a *carrier*. The device then waits a short period of time and checks again.

> *Note: The use of the term* carrier *in this case is not the same as the carrier signal used by modems. A modem carrier is a tone of a known frequency, which is raised or lowered during data transmission to indicate patterns of 0s and 1s. Ethernet uses the term merely to indicate the presence of a signal on the network.*

If the network is idle (no carrier is detected), then the device begins transmitting its frame. But what if two devices checked the network at exactly the same time, each determined that the network was idle, and then transmitted a frame at exactly the same time? This situation is known as a *collision*, and it does occur with some regularity.

The Ethernet hardware can detect a collision. In that case, a device waits a random amount of time and attempts the transmission again, first rechecking to see if the network is idle. Assuming that the random wait interval is different for the two colliding devices, it is unlikely the same collision will occur again for the same frames.

This scheme for regulating network traffic is known as *Carrier Sense Multiple Access with Collision Detection* (CSMA/CD). The "carrier sense" portion, of course, refers to a device's ability to sense the presence of a frame on the network. The "multiple access" portion represents the idea that all devices on the network have equal access to the transmission media. Finally, "collision detection" describes a device's ability to detect a collision and handle the situation.

Each bus to which nodes are attached constitutes a *collision domain* (or a *network segment*, in more general terminology). All nodes within a single collision domain are therefore contending for access to the same network transmission medium. Large Ethernet networks are assembled by connecting individual collision domains using hardware such as switches, routers, and bridges. You will read about this interconnection hardware in Chapter 5.

The more devices there are in a collision domain and the more frames they are sending (the heavier the traffic), the more likely collisions are to occur. In a very busy, heavily loaded collision domain, a collision may occur repeatedly for the same frame. Users will detect this as a general slowdown in the network. It may mean that you need to reexamine the way in which the network is laid out; breaking it into smaller collision domains or upgrading the type of Ethernet in use may be warranted.

Because only one signal can be on the transmission media at one time, Ethernet networks are *half-duplex* (transmission in only one direction at a time). This is in contrast, for example, to *full-duplex* telephone transmissions, where signals travel in two directions at once. (You may have trouble hearing what is being said if you are talking at the same time as the person on the other end of the phone call, but the technology nonetheless supports full-duplex operations.)

> *Note: It is possible to configure Ethernet for full-duplex operations. However, to do so two devices must be connected directly*

to one another, without any other devices on the network. They must also use cabling that has at least two transmission paths (two or more wires or multiple optical fibers) because the simultaneous signals must travel on different media.

Alternative Ethernet Topologies

As you read earlier, technically all Ethernets use a bus topology. However, at first glance some may seem to use *star* or *daisy-chain* topologies.

The Star Topology

A star topology has a single central device to which all other devices in the network are connected. In the simplest configuration, the device at the center is a *hub* that does nothing but pass signals through its internal wiring.

From the outside, a star topology looks something like Figure 2-3. Each device, which is connected to the hub, sends frames to the hub, which then directs them to the correct receiving device.

In reality, the hub is not really a traffic director, but a hiding place for a foreshortened bus. In you look at Figure 2-4, for example, you can see how the bus is hidden inside a hub. The cable coming from each device is attached to the hub via a *port* or *MAU* (medium attachment unit), which in turn is wired to the bus. Because the bus and the direct connections to the bus are hidden within the hub's casing, the configuration has the external appearance of a star.

> *Note: If you have worked in a Token Ring networking environment, then you may run across a different meaning for the acronym MAU: multiple attachment unit. In a Token Ring network, a MAU is a box to which devices connect, forming the ring. A Token Ring MAU is therefore the equivalent of an Ethernet hub.*

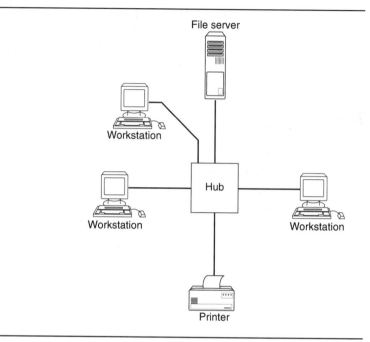

Figure 2-3:   A simple star topology for an Ethernet network

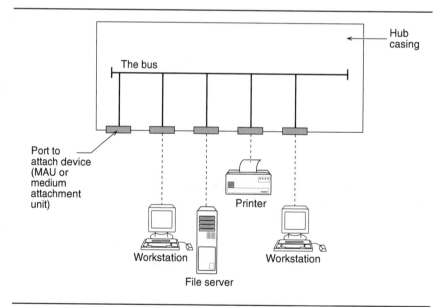

Figure 2-4:   A bus hidden inside a hub

The type of hub you use in a star topology, how many ports it has, how the hubs can be connected together, and the capabilities of the hub vary depending on the type of Ethernet you are using. You will learn more about the choices you have throughout this book.

The Daisy-Chain Topology

A daisy-chain topology is one in which the bus is formed by connecting devices in a chain, as in Figure 2-5. Although this may at first look similar to the simple bus in Figure 2-2, keep in mind that in this case, the bus is not a single, unbroken medium. Instead, a daisy-chainable adapter is connected to each device. Then the adapters are connected by individual cable segments.

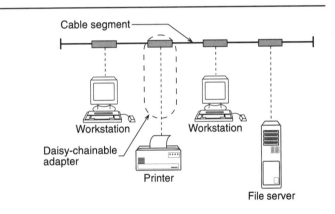

Figure 2-5:   A daisy-chain topology

Media and Ethernet Standards

The IEEE has organized the Ethernet standards around both speed and type of transmission media. You can find an overview of the most commonly used standards in Table 2-1.

The naming of the standards is not quite as strange as may first appear. The number at the left of the name indicates the speed of the

Standard	Speed	Transmission media
10BASE5	10 Mbps	Thick coaxial cable
10BASE2	10 Mbps	Thin coaxial cable
10BROAD36	10 Mbps	Thick coaxial cable
10BASE-T	10 Mbps	Twisted-pair wire
10BASE-F	10 Mbps	Fiber optic cable
100BASE-TX	100 Mbps	Twisted-pair wire[a]
100BASE-FX	100 Mbps	Fiber optic cable
1000BASE-CX	1 Gbps	Short copper cable[b]
1000BASE-LX	1 Gbps	Long-wavelength fiber optic cable
1000BASE-SX	1 Gbps	Short-wavelength fiber optic cable

Table 2-1: IEEE Ethernet standards

[a] All Fast Ethernet standards are referred to as 100BASE-T. 100BASE-X is a subset of that standard. 100BASE-TX and 100BASE-FX are subsets of 100BASE-X.

[b] All Gigabit Ethernet standards are referred to as 1000BASE-T. 1000BASE-X is a subset of that standard. 1000BASE-CX, 1000BASE-LX, and 1000BASE-SX are subsets of 1000BASE-X.

standards in megabits per second. The number or letter at the end is related to the maximum length of a single piece of cable. For example, the 5 at the end of 10BASE5 stands for 500 meters; the T at the end of 10BASE-T stands for 100 meters.

The word *BASE* in most of the names refers to *baseband*. Baseband media carry one signal at a time. The opposite is *broadband*, media that carry more than one signal at a time. Although there is a standard for 10 Mbps broadband Ethernet, it is no longer widely used. (You may run into some older networks—those installed in the 1980s—that do use broadband technology, however.)

There may appear to be one rather glaring omission from the standards: wireless media. In fact, wireless transmissions integrate into existing Ethernet cable-based networks and are typically compatible with 10BASE-T, 10BASE-2, 100BASE-TX, and 100BASE-FX. Wireless transmissions therefore do not represent a distinct Ethernet standard. (You will read more about the use of wireless devices in Chapter 6.)

Part Two

Transmission Media and Network Connections

Today's computer networks employ several types of communications media: wire of various sizes and materials, fiber optics, and wireless transmissions. Each of the Ethernet standards developed by the IEEE uses a different kind of media. This means that when you choose a transmission medium, you are also to some extent limiting the type of Ethernet you can use. The converse is also true: When you commit to a type of Ethernet, you may also be restricting which media you can use.

In this part of the book we will examine network media used to create individual network segments (collision domains), looking at their transmission speeds, the distances over which they are useful, how devices are connected to the network, and so on. You will also see how the various IEEE Ethernet standards are tied to types of media. Then we will consider how you connect the individual sections into larger networks and look at how wireless transmissions can be integrated in an Ethernet network.

3

Standard (10 Mbps) Ethernet

Although prices for Fast (100 Mbps) Ethernet have decreased dramatically recently, standard 10 Mbps Ethernet is still widely used for small networks because it is very inexpensive and relatively easy to install and maintain.

Standard (10 Mbps) Ethernet can travel over four different types of media: twisted-pair wire, fiber optic cable, thin coaxial cable, and thick coaxial cable. There are many factors involved in choosing a type of cabling, including physical malleability of the cabling (can it be bent?), cost to purchase and install, bandwidth, and segment length. You will read about all of these factors in this chapter and the next.

Twisted-Pair Wire (10BASE-T)

The most commonly used cabling for standard Ethernet today is twisted-pair wire (10BASE-T). It is inexpensive and easy to set up and maintain. In most cases, twisted-pair wire networks require hubs and use the pseudo-star configuration described in Chapter 2.

Twisted-pair wire cables contain one or more pairs of copper wires that are twisted in a spiral manner. For example, the cable in Figure 3-1 has four pairs of wires. Because the cable itself includes no shielding, this type of cable is called *unshielded twisted pair* (UTP).

Figure 3-1: Twisted-pair wire cabling (courtesy of Belden Wire & Cable Co.)

UTP Cabling

The Electronics Industries Association (EIA) has set standards for the quality of UTP cabling: Category 3, Category 4, and Category 5. The major difference between them is the number of twists in each pair of wires. For example, Category 4 cabling has three or four twists per *foot*, whereas Category 5 cabling has three or four twists per *inch*. (The illustration in Figure 3-1 is Category 5 cable.)

Why is this twisting important? Because when you bundle multiple pairs of wires in the same cable, the signals tend to bleed from one pair to another (*crosstalk*). The twisting of the pairs reduces the crosstalk and therefore the amount of *noise* (unwanted signal) affecting each transmission traveling down the cable, which in turn helps to reduce transmission errors.

Category 3 cabling is the standard voice-grade twisted-pair cable that carries telephone transmissions. (The typical telephone cable has two pairs of wires and can therefore carry two telephone lines.) Because it is already installed in most buildings, it can be attractive to consider employing unused telephone lines to carry 10BASE-T network signals. However, Category 3 cable is designed to carry signals at a maximum speed of only 16 Mbps, restricting its use to 10 Mbps Ethernet.

Virtually all of today's new 10BASE-T installations use Category 5 cabling, which can carry signals traveling at up to 100 Mbps. Given that Category 5 cabling is relatively inexpensive, there is no reason to use cabling of any lesser quality when installing new wiring for a network or during new construction.

If you are installing cables inside walls, heating/air-conditioning ducts, or other spaces where the air is breathed by people, then you will need to use what is known as *plenum* wiring. Plenum cables have a plastic coating that is less toxic when burned than standard cabling. It costs a little more, but is required by most building codes.

The UTP wire used in 10BASE-T networks connects to a devices network interface card (for an example, see Figure 3-2) and to the network itself with an RJ-45 connector. As you can see in Figure 3-3, it appears to be a larger cousin of the RJ-11 connectors used in modular telephone systems.

Note: The acronym RJ stands for registered jack.

UTP Cabling Lengths

Each piece of UTP cabling connecting a device to a hub must be no longer than 100 meters. The reasons behind this lie in the properties of the copper wire used in the cables.

> ♦ *Attenuation:* As signals travel over a piece of copper wire, they lose strength due to friction on the surface of the wire (*attenuation*). This effect becomes progressively worse with distance.

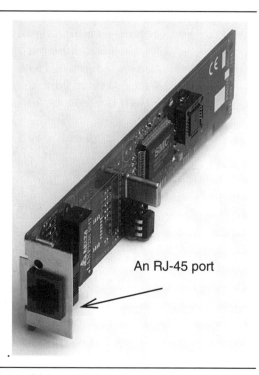

Figure 3-2:   A port on an NIC into which an RJ-11 connector is plugged
(courtesy of Farallon Corp.)

Figure 3-3:   RJ-45 connectors (courtesy of Belkin)

♦ *Interference:* Interference from outside sources—for example, the crosstalk described earlier or other electrical
sources in the environment—can change signal strength
and type, introducing errors into transmissions. The effect of interference becomes worse the longer a signal is
exposed to possible sources of interference. Therefore,
longer cable runs are more suspectible to interference
than are shorter lengths of cable.

♦ *Noise:* Noise (any unwanted signal) on the wire also introduces errors and becomes worse over time (and therefore distance).

Research has shown that these problems are kept to an acceptable level when the maximum length of a single piece of UTP cable is 100 meters.

UTP Jack Wiring

The jacks that you saw in Figure 3-3 are actually part of a four-member group of modular jacks. The 8-position jacks at the top of Figure 3-4 are among those we sometimes call RJ-45 connectors. The 6-position jacks at the bottom of Figure 3-4 are the RJ-11 jacks usually found with Category 3 telephone wire.

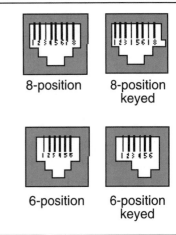

8-position   8-position
                 keyed

6-position   6-position
                 keyed

Figure 3-4: Modular jack types (courtesy of The Siemon Company)

To be technically correct, however, calling these jacks simply RJ-45 and RJ-11 is a bit misleading because the RJ designation refers to how the jacks are wired as well as to their physical shape. The jack wiring specifications for three of the jacks (all except the 6-position keyed) are part of the Universal Service Ordering Codes (USOC). For example, the USOC codes include the following specifications:

- ♦ RJ11C: A 6-position jack using only one pair of wires. (Not illustrated in Figure 3-4.)
- ♦ RJ14C: A 6-position jack using two pairs of wires. This is the wiring typically used for household telephones; each cable has four wires and can support two telephone lines. Its wiring diagram appears at the bottm left of Figure 3-4.
- ♦ RJ25C: A 6-position jack using three pairs of wires. (Not illustrated in Figure 3-4.)
- ♦ RJ61C: An 8-position jack using four pairs of wires. The wiring diagram can be found at the top left of Figure 3-4.

The 8-position keyed jack also has USOC standards. However, the 6-position keyed jack was developed by Digital and is used only for their equipment.

Just because two cables have the same jack does not mean they are wired in the same way. You must, of course, match the wiring of the cable to the port into which it will be plugged. A typical 10BASE-T cable uses an 8-position jack but only two pairs of wires, as in Figure 3-5. This is the wiring that we usually mean when we say"RJ-45."

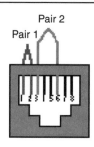

Figure 3-5:   10BASE-T jack wiring (courtesy of The Siemon Company)

Note: We will revisit this issue of cable, port, and wall outlet wiring when we talk about structured cabling systems in Chapter 5.

Creating 10BASE-T Network Segments Using a Hub

Simple 10BASE-T networks almost always use a hub like that in Figure 3-6, producing the typical star configuration. An RJ-45 connector snaps into place in the hub just like an RJ-11 telephone connector. Connecting a small 10BASE-T network therefore requires nothing more than snapping cables into the network interfaces of the devices to be connected to the network and snapping the other ends of those cables into the hub's ports.

Figure 3-6:   10BASE-T hub (courtesy of 3Com Corporation)

If a NIC or the Ethernet hardware on a motherboard doesn't have an RJ-45 port, but instead has either an *AUI* (attachment unit interface) or *AAUI* (Apple attachment unit interface) port, you can still use that device on a 10BASE-T network by connecting the device first to a 10BASE-T transceiver such as that in Figure 3-7.

The transceiver, connected to the device via a transceiver cable, acts as a converter between the AUI or AAUI port and an RJ-45 port. It also ensures that the device receives the same type of signal, regardless of the type of Ethernet cabling in use.

> Note: Most RJ-45-equipped NICs do not require external transceivers because the circuitry contained in a transceiver is built into the NIC.

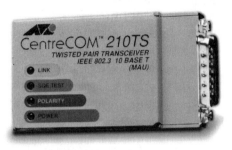

Figure 3-7: A 10BASE-T transceiver (courtesy of Allied Telesyn)

In Figure 3-8 you will find a summary of the ways in which you typically attach devices to a 10BASE-T hub. Notice that some devices use a NIC, some use a NIC and a transceiver, while still others have all networking hardware (including the transceiver) built onto the motherboard.

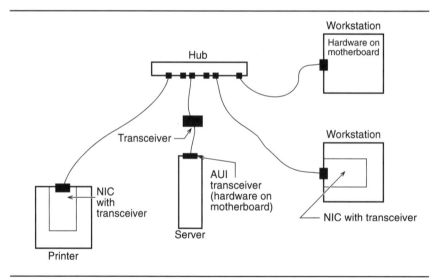

Figure 3-8: Constructing a 10BASE-T network using a hub

An alternative to a desktop hub—often used in multifloor office buildings—is a *wiring closet,* a locked cabinet that contains the wiring for the bus. All devices are connected to the bus inside the wiring closet. The wiring closet also typically contains hardware that connects the bus on a single floor with other networks in the building. (You will read more about connecting multiple Ethernet segments into larger networks in Chapter 5.)

> *Note: Wiring closets are locked for security purposes. Anyone with access to the bus itself can easily tap into the network by simply plugging in a computer.*

The Daisy-Chain Alternative

If you are creating a very small network—eight nodes or less—then you can assemble a 10BASE-T network by daisy-chaining the devices using EtherWave connectors (products of Farallon), as in Figure 3-9. Although EtherWave does let you create a 10BASE-T network without a hub, the price of a passive, unmanaged eight-port hub is under $100. If you need to network more than two or three devices and the devices have built-in 10BASE-T interfaces, then it is probably cheaper to purchase a hub.

However, EtherWave has one major advantage: The manufacturer makes adapters for hardware (printers and computers, primarily) that do not have expansion slots for network interface cards. Nonetheless, an EtherWave adapter can be used with a hub so that you can integrate the adapter with a hub-centered configuration should a very small network become too large for EtherWave.

Fiber Optics (10BASE-F)

Fiber optic cable is made up of a collection of glass tubes spun as thin as hairs. Each tube can carry a single pulse of light that represents one bit in a data transmission. By bundling many of these fibers together, a single cable can transmit many bits at the same time. In a simple fiber optic cable, such as that in Figure 3-10, the optical fibers are surrounded by a semirigid material that gives the cable strength and protects the fibers within is in turn encased in a protective outer jacket (see Figure 3-11).

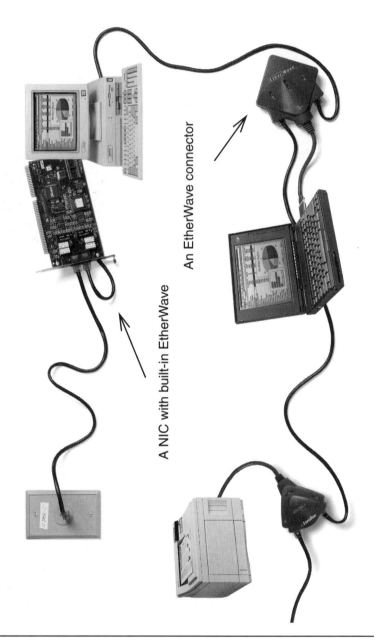

Figure 3-9:   An EtherWave daisy chain (Used with permission of Farallon Corp.)

Figure 3-10:   Fiber optic cable (courtesy of Belden Wire & Cable Co.)

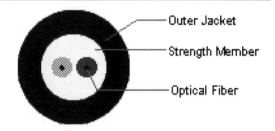

Figure 3-11:   The construction of a fiber optic cable (courtesy of Belden Wire & Cable Co.)

The use of fiber optic cable has some very significant advantages.

- ◆ Because it uses light rather than electrical signals to transmit data, it is invulnerable to electrical interference, crosstalk, and attenuation. Fiber optic media can therefore be used in situations where wire media pose problems, such as on factory floors.
- ◆ It is much harder for someone to tap than wire media.
- ◆ It has much higher bandwidth than most wire media. The same fiber optic media can carry 10 Mbs, Fast Ethernet, and Gigabit Ethernet signals.

On the other hand, fiber optic cabling is more difficult to work with than wire. It cannot be spliced and taped with electrical tape like wire, but instead requires special connectors that precisely line up the ends of two segments of cable with one another. In addition, fiber optic equipment is more expensive than equipment for wire media.

Nonetheless, in environments where the amount of data traffic is expected to grow beyond what standard Ethernet can handle or where severe electrical interference is a factor, fiber optic cabling is a viable choice. For example, in graphics and video design firms where large files move between workstations, fiber optic cabling can significantly speed up workflow.

The original fiber optic standard (FOIRL) was designed for the use of fiber optic cabling only between Ethernet segments, linking them with repeaters. (A *repeater* is a piece of hardware that amplifies and retransmits a network signal; repeater capabilities are built into even the simples of hubs.) However, the standard has been extended to include using fiber optic cabling to connect devices directly to a network (in particular, 10BASE-FL).

> *Note: Both FOIRL and 10BASE-FL are subsets of the 10BASE-F standard.*

10BASE-FL supports segments up to 2,000 meters long. However, if FOIRL equipment is also present on the network, a segment is limited to 1,000 meters.

Like 10BASE-T, 10BASE-FL requires a hub. To connect a device to a standard Ethernet network using 10BASE-FL, you need a 10BASE-FL transceiver that is connected to an AUI or AAUI port on a NIC (or part of the motherboard's hardware.) Unlike other Ethernet connections, however, the fiber optic transceiver has two cables running to a hub rather than one. One cable carries data being transmitted; the other carries data being received.

To make the hookup to the hub, you connect the transmit line from the transceiver to a receive port on the hub. You then connect the receive line from the transceiver to the transmit port on the hub. (This is directly analogous to the way in which you make audio or video connections in your home: Cables run from the "out" port on one device to the "in" port on another.)

You will find a diagram of some sample fiber optic connections in Figure 3-12. Notice that for those devices in which transceiver hardware is not part of a NIC (or on the motherboard), there is a single transceiver cable running between the device and the fiber optic transceiver. The receive and transmit cables then run from the transceiver to the fiber optic repeater hub.

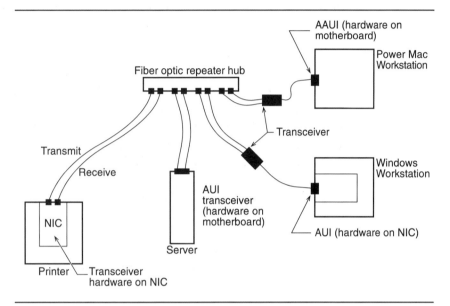

Figure 3-12:   Constructing a 10 Mbps network using fiber optic cable

Note: For additional information about types of fiber optic cabling and the relationship between type of cable and segment length, see page 58.

Thin Coaxial Cable (10BASE2)

Prior to the relatively recent popularity of 10BASE-T and UTP wiring, most Ethernet networks were constructed using thin coaxial cable (thinnet or 10BASE2), such as that in Figure 3-13. Although it looks like the cable you use to connect your VCR to your TV set, the electrical characteristics of the cable and the connector are different.

Figure 3-13:   Thin coaxial cable (courtesy of Belden Wire & Cable Co.)

As you can see in Figure 3-13, coaxial cable is made up of several layers. A copper wire runs down the center, surrounded by a sheath of plastic insulation. The plastic is covered by a foil shield, which in turn is covered by a braided-copper mesh. The outer covering is plastic, which protects the cable from the elements. The connectors placed on the end of the cable make contact with both the inner copper wire and the braided-copper mesh.

10BASE2 does not require a hub like 10BASE-T. Instead, devices are connected to the network using transceivers and a transceiver cable, as in Figure 3-14. The transceiver is a separate unit (see Figure 3-15).

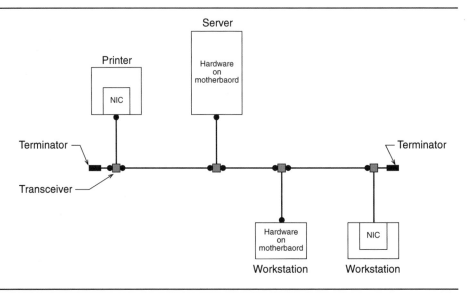

Figure 3-14:   Connecting devices to create a 10BASE2 network

Figure 3-15:   A 10BASE2 transceiver (courtesy of Allied Telesyn)

Thinnet networks typically use BNC connectors such as that in Figure 3-16. The outer sleeve of the connector rotates to snap into place, making a firm connection between the cable the transceiver or NIC to which it is being attached (see Figure 3-17). (Many RGB monitors also use BNC connectors to connect individual red, green, and blue cables.)

Figure 3-16:   BNC connector (Courtesy of Belkin)

Note: There seems to be some disagreement over what BNC stands for. Some people think it means British Naval Connector, while others think it means Bayonet Neill-Concelman. (Neill and Concelman designed the connectors.) And yet still others insist that the meaning is Barrel Nut Connector. Take your pick …

Like a 10BASE-T network, a 10BASE2 network is made up of short segments of cable. The bus is assembled by connecting lengths of

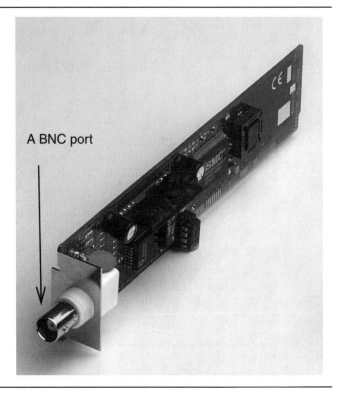

Figure 3-17:   A BNC port on a NIC (courtesy of Farallon Corp.)

coax with BNC tee connectors (see Figure 3-18). You need one tee connector at each point to which a device is connected to the network. A piece of network cable attaches at each end of the tee's crossbar; a transceiver cable connects to the "leg" of the tee.

10BASE2 network segments also require *terminators* at each end (see Figure 3-19). A terminator acts to prevent the unwanted reflection of signals from the ends of the bus back down the network medium. You can either put a separate terminator like that in on each end of the cable, or you can purchase tee connectors that are self-terminating and use the self-terminating tee connectors for the last device on each end of the cable.

Thin coax is relatively inexpensive and, as you might guess by the name of the IEEE standard that describes it, can handle segment

Figure 3-18:   A BNC tee connector (courtesy of Belkin)

Figure 3-19:   10BASE2 cable terminator (courtesy of Belkin)

lengths of up to 200 meters. It also bends easily and therefore lends itself to being installed in walls, ceilings, and across floors to be connected directly to network devices. In addition, it has the benefit of not requiring a hub.

However, the flexibility of UTP wire and the ability to use existing wiring has resulted in fewer and fewer new 10BASE2 networks being installed. Thin coax is also limited to 10 Mbps second, while Category 5 UTP wire can carry 100 Mbps as well.

It may be tempting to use thin coax for a small network (10 or fewer nodes), in particular because the cable, NICs, and connectors are inexpensive. However, when the network grows beyond a single room or more than 10 nodes, coax is not a good choice. The cable is very hard to bend and the connectors are quite fragile. Coupled with the fact that coax cannot support anything faster than 10 Mps, coax should probably not be used for a new network.

Thick Coaxial Cable (10BASE5)

The original DIX Ethernet standard and the first IEEE standard (10BASE5) was written for thick coaxial cable, such as that in Figure 3-20. Although a single piece of cable can be up to 500 meters long without running into signal problems, thick coax is physically hard to bend, simply because it is so thick. In fact, its diameter is about a half-inch. Although you can't tell from the black-and-white illustration, its typical bright yellow outer coating has given thick coax its nickname of "frozen yellow garden hose."

Figure 3-20:   Thick coaxial cable (courtesy of Belden Wire & Cable Co.)

The basic technique for creating 10BASE5 networks was to install a *drop cable* made up of a single, unbroken stretch of thick coaxial cable. Then, each device was equipped with a NIC that had an AUI to which a transceiver cable was attached. The other end of the transceiver cable was attached to the transceiver, which in turn clamped onto the drop cable.

In early implementations, the transceiver actually cut through the outer wrappings of the drop cable to make physical contact with the copper mesh layer and the copper wire at the center (a "vampire clamp," such as the one used by the transceiver in Figure 3-21). This meant that if you disconnected a transceiver from the drop cable, you were left with a break in the cable's shielding.

Figure 3-21:   A 10BASE5 transceiver that uses a vampire clamp to tap into thicknet cable (courtesy of Allied TeleSyn)

Because 10BASE5 is so difficult to work with, it is no longer being used in new networks. However, there are many 10BASE5 *backbones* (networks to which other networks are connected) still in use in office parks and college campuses today, and it is still possible to get replacement parts (cables and transceivers) for such networks.

4

Fast and Gigabit Ethernet

The Fast (100 Mbps) and Gigabit (1000 Mbps) Ethernet standards specify the use of either twisted-pair wire or fiber optic media. Where UTP is concerned, you will see that the Fast Ethernet standards are more precise about the type of media than are those for standard Ethernet. The hardware used for connecting devices to a network is also somewhat different.

Fast Ethernet Media

There are actually four Fast Ethernet media specifications, three of which use UTP wire and one of which uses fiber optic cable. All Fast Ethernet networks require a hub that contains the bus wiring, just like the 10BASE-T hubs you read about in Chapter 3. Such hubs amplify and then broadcast the signal throughout the bus.

Note: As you will read in Chapter 5, the situation with hubs is not as clear cut as it might at first appear. You can purchase a single hub, for example, that supports both 10 Mbps and 100 Mbps Ethernet connections. In addition, there are several varieties of hubs and a number of limitations on how they can be used in a Fast Ethernet system.

Twisted-Pair Wire

The three Fast Ethernet options that are designed for UTP wire are summarized in Table 4-1. Current installations, however, are almost exclusively 100BASE-TX, using Category 5 wire. We will therefore be focusing solely on 100BASE-TX.

Standard	Cable type
100BASE-TX	Category 5 UTP (uses 2 pairs of wires)
100BASE-T4	Category 3 UTP (uses 4 pairs of wires)
100BASE-T2	Category 3 UTP (uses 2 pairs of wires)

Table 4-1:   Fast Ethernet cabling options

In concept, a Fast Ethernet connection is very similar to a standard Ethernet connection, although the equipment is slightly different. You can attach a device using an external transceiver (see Figure 4-1) or using a NIC that contains the transceiver (see Figure 4-2).

Notice that in Figure 4-1 there are specific names attached to each part of the connection. These names, and their acronyms, are actually part of the 100BASE-T standard. Given that the acronyms actually show up in product literature, it will be easier to specify what you need (and to understand what someone is trying to sell you) if you have at least a basic understanding of what they mean.

The term *data terminal equipment* (DTE) comes from the very earliest days of computing, when dumb terminals connected to host mainframes were the only way to interact with a computer. Today, a DTE is any device that you are going to connect to a network.

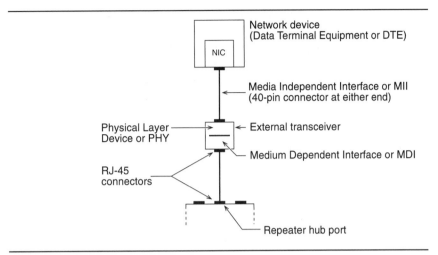

Figure 4-1: **Connecting a device to a 100BASE-TX network using an external transceiver**

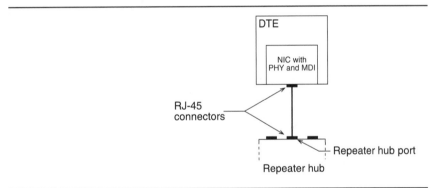

Figure 4-2: **Connecting a device to a 100BASE-TX network using a NIC that contains transceiver hardware**

If you are using an external transceiver, then you connect it to a NIC in your device with a *media independent interface* (MII), a cable that has a 40-pin connector at either end. The transceiver itself contains the *Physical layer device* (PHY) and also the *medium dependent interface* (MDI), which terminates in an RJ-45 port. The final connection to the repeater hub is made by connecting the UTP cable to the port on the transceiver and to a port on the hub.

If, however, you have purchased a NIC that contains transceiver hardware (the MII, PHY, and MDI), then the NIC will have an RJ-45 port like that in Figure 4-3. All you need to do is plug an RJ-45 connector into the NIC and the other end of the cable into the repeater hub.

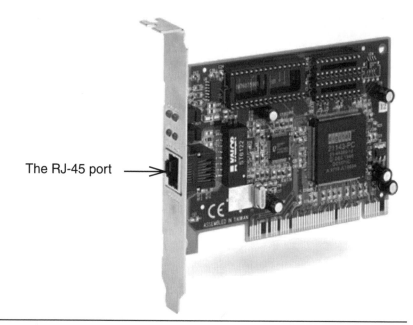

The RJ-45 port

Figure 4-3:   A 10/100 NIC that includes transceiver hardware (courtesy of Farallon Corp.)

Note: The NIC in Figure 4-3 can handle both standard and Fast Ethernet connections. This is a very typical configuration today.

Fiber Optics

Fiber optic configurations for Fast Ethernet are covered by the 100BASE-FX standard. Like standard Ethernet wiring for fiber optic cables, Fast Ethernet fiber optics requires two cables, one for transmitting and one for receiving. A connection can be made through an external transceiver, in which case an MII sits between the 40-pin connectors on the NIC and the transceiver. Alternatively, you can use a NIC that contains the transceiver.

In either case, connections are made to a fiber optic repeater hub using two cables rather than one (see Figure 4-4 and Figure 4-5).

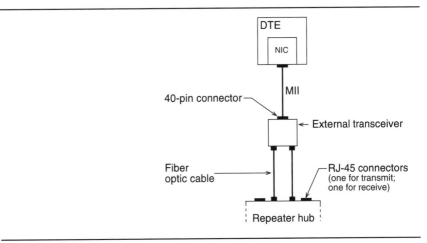

Figure 4-4:   Connecting to a 100BASE-FX network segment using an external transceiver

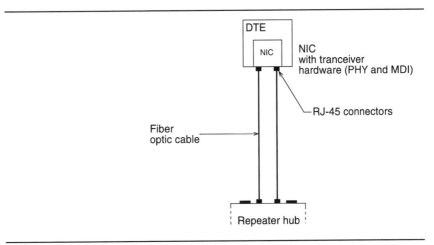

Figure 4-5:   Connecting to a 100BASE-FX network segment using a NIC containing transceiver hardware

Gigabit Ethernet Media

At the time this book was written, Gigabit Ethernet was viewed primarily as suitable only for servers. The idea is that you place a Gigabit Ethernet NIC in one or more servers and then connect the servers to fiber optic media. Other network segments (either standard Ethernet or Fast Ethernet) connect to the fiber optic cable. The intent is therefore to speed up access to servers, rather than to speed the transmissions from individual workstations.

> *Note: For information on interconnecting Ethernet segments, see Chapter 5.*

Like Fast Ethernet, the Gigabit Ethernet standard has been written for two types of media: fiber optics and copper wire.

Fiber Optics

There are actually three standards that deal with Gigabit Ethernet networks built from fiber optic cable.

- *1000BASE-CX*: Designed for the direct interconnection of clusters of equipment.
- *1000BASE-SX*: Designed for horizontal cabling.
- *1000BASE-LX*: Designed for interconnecting network segments, including vertical runs through buildings.

The distance that you can run a fiber optic segment depends on the diameter of the fibers in the cable and the cable's bandwidth. As you can see in Table 4-2, segment lengths vary from 230 to 5000 meters. There is, however, a large gap between the last entry in the table (5000-meter maximum) and the remaining entries. The reason for this discrepancy lies with the type of fiber optic cable being used.

With the exception of the last entry in the table (a *single-mode* cable), all of the cables are *multimode*. When light enters a multimode fiber

Standard	Diameter (in microns)	Bandwidth (MHz*km)	Cable length (in meters)
1000BASE-SX	62.5	160	2 – 230
	62.5	200	2 – 275
	50	400	2 – 500
	50	500	2 – 550
1000BASE-LX	62.5	500	2 – 550
	50	400	2 – 550
	50	500	2 – 550
	9	n/a	2 – 5000
	5	5000	2 – 5000

Table 4-2:   Sample fiber optic cable lengths

optic cable, light rays that strike the fiber at a shallow angle are re-flected and therefore propagated down the cable. Other light rays are absorbed by the surrounding material. The term *multimode* refers to the fact that light arriving at more than one angle will be reflected.

Each angle of reflection has a different transmission speed. There-fore, the data do not arrive at their destination at a constant rate. This slows down the accurate reception of data because the receiving device must account for an irregular arrival pattern. In addition, the possibility for distortion of the signal increases with distance, limiting the length of a network segment.

However, if you significantly reduce the diameter of the optical fiber (for example, down to 9 or 5 microns as in Table 4-2), then you reduce the number of angles at which light will reflect to only one. This is single-mode transmission, in which all bits travel at more or less the same speed, making it easier to more accurately detect incoming signals. In addition, there is far less chance for signal distortion. The length of a segment can therefore be considerably longer than with multimode cable.

Note: Another benefit of single-mode fiber optic cable is that its smaller fiber diameter means that more fibers can be bundled into less space than with multimode cable.

As mentioned earlier, Gigabit Ethernet is currently being used to connect servers to a Gigabit Ethernet hub or switch (for an example, see Figure 4-6). To make the connection, you place a Gigabit Ethernet NIC in the server and then connect it to the switch using a cable terminated with a Gigabit Ethernet connector. The NIC in Figure 4-7, for example, is a 1000BASE-SX card.

Figure 4-6:   A Gigabit Ethernet hub (courtesy of 3Com Corporation)

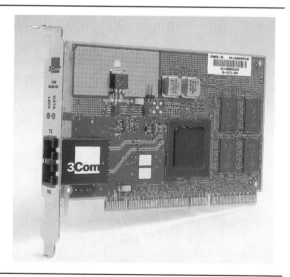

Figure 4-7:   A Gigabit Ethernet NIC (coutesy of 3Com Corporation)

Note: In both Figure 4-6 and Figure 4-7 there are two connectors for each port. This is because the hardware is intended for fiber optic cabling, which, as you may remember from earlier in this chapter, requires two cables, one for the input signal and one for the output signal.

Twisted-Pair Wire

Although the Gigabit Ethernet standard includes 1000BASE-T for Category 5 UTP wire, at the time this book went to press (spring 1999), specifications for that standard had not been completed and therefore no equipment to support Gigabit Ethernet over UTP was available.

However, Intel and Level One, a manufacturer of networking components, began working together in July 1998 to build equipment for UTP wire. They were also working closely with the IEEE committee that was writing standard specifications. Given that the IEEE hoped to have the specifications approved by the second quarter of 1999 and that Intel and Level One expected to ship equipment on or before that date, you theoretically should be able to find some UTP NICs, hubs, and switches that will support Gigabit Ethernet.

The major advantage of using UTP over fiber optic cabling is price. Expect to find the UTP equipment as much as 50 percent cheaper than equipment for fiber optics. As a result, Gigabit Ethernet may begin to make sense for use in workstations as well as servers.

5

Connecting Network Segments

To this point, we have looked primarily at creating single network segments. However, unless you have a very small office, you will probably need to connect multiple segments into a larger network. In this chapter we will therefore look at the hardware and cabling necessary to construct larger, expandable networks.

Interconnection Hardware

There are many devices that can be used to create multiple-segment networks, including hubs, switches, routers, bridges, and gateways. The best starting point for this discussion is therefore a look at the differences between these types of hardware and the uses for which they are best suited.

63

Hubs (Repeaters)

As you know, a hub (also known as a *repeater* or a *repeater hub*) is a device that contains the wiring of a bus. You plug network devices into ports on the hub to connect them to the bus. At their simplest, hubs are not strictly segment interconnection hardware, given that you need a hub to create a single 10BASE-T or Fast Ethernet segment. However, hubs can be used to create larger segments.

10BASE-T Unmanaged Hubs

The simplest type of hub is an *unmanaged hub* or *passive hub*. Used primarily with UTP and fiber optic networks, unmanaged hubs accept an incoming signal, amplify it, and broadcast it to all devices on the network, just as would happen if the networked devices were plugged directly into a bus cable. The important thing to understand here is that all devices connected to the hub receive the signal. As with a 10BASE2 or 10BASE5 network configured without a hub, each device must examine the destination address in each transmitted frame to determine if it is the intended recipient of the message.

Unmanaged hubs (such as the the 24-port hub in Figure 5-1) are inexpensive, as low as $50 for an eight-port 10BASE-T hub at the time this book was written. They are also very easy to set up and use. To create a network segment, you plug the hub into an electrical outlet, plug UTP cables into the network devices, and plug UTP cables into the hub. That is all there is to the physical setup!

Most unmanaged hubs are designed to be daisy-chained together to create larger networks. To make this possible, each hub has an extra port. For example, an eight-port hub designed for daisy chaining will actually have nine ports. The extra port is designed to be connected to another hub with a 10BASE-T cable joining the individual network segments into a single network. When the ninth port is used to connect to another hub, the eighth port on the hub cannot be used to connect a network device. In some cases, you may also find that the "extra" port is an AUI, AAUI, or BNC port rather than a 10BASE-T port.

Figure 5-1:   A 24-port unmanaged hub (courtesy of 3Com Corporation)

The extra port in an unmanaged hub has some special electrical properties: It is a *crossover port* in which the transmit and receive wires are reversed. This is essential so that the two hubs do not attempt to send and receive on the same wires. In fact, you can use any of the other ports in an unmanaged hub to connect to another hub *if* you use a *crossover cable,* a cable where the transmit and receive wires are reversed at one end.

> *Note: You may also encounter hubs with a BNC connector for interconnecting hubs rather than an extra RJ-45 port. You would then use coaxial cable to interconnect two hubs, making it possible for you to use all the RJ-45 ports in the hub. Some hubs also have AUI connectors that can be used with fiber optic converters to connect hubs to a backbone or to connect hubs between buildings.*

It might appear that you could connect an infinite number of hubs in this way. However, the maximum distance between any two devices on a 10BASE-T network is 500 meters. For example, in Figure 5-2, if all of the cable lengths are 100 meters, then the maximum number of network segments is four, because the distance between the two farthest workstations is 500 meters.

In addition to the maximum distance between devices, you must also ensure that a 10BASE-T network is a true daisy chain, that it does not contain any loops. If a loop occurs, signals will be retransmitted forever around the loop because there would be no end to the bus. The configuration in Figure 5-3(a) is acceptable because

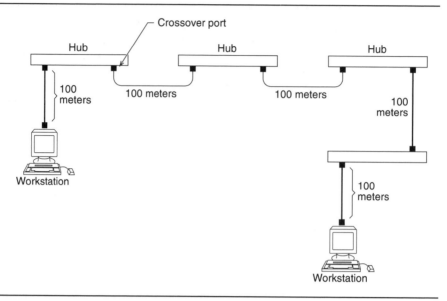

Figure 5-2:   A daisy-chained 10BASE-T network

there are ends to the bus. However, the configuration in Figure 5-3(b) will not work because it contains a loop.

Unmanaged hubs come in a variety of sizes, from 5 to 24 ports. Coupled with the limit on the length of 10BASE-T cable, you can see that a 10BASE-T network that uses only unmanaged hubs cannot grow to be very large.

All the devices connected into a network by unmanaged hubs are part of a single collision domain, all of which are contending for access to a single bus at the same time. When there are 24 devices attempting to communicate simultaneously (something that would rarely happen in practice in a small network), performance still remains very good. However, as the size of the network increases, performance will suffer. In fact, when a single collision domain grows to around 200 devices, the network collapses during high traffic periods, unable to transmit acceptably clear signals.

Therefore, the maximum cable length is not as much of a limitation as it might seem. To obtain acceptable performance with a larger

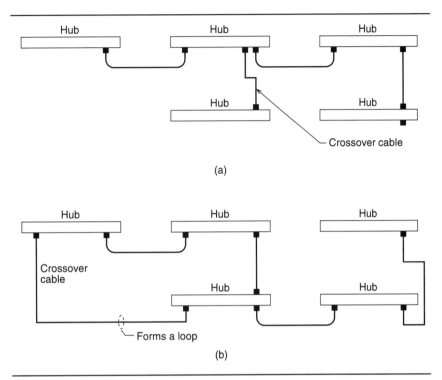

Figure 5-3: Correct and incorrect 10BASE-T hub interconnections

Ethernet network, you will need to connect the network with something that breaks it into multiple collision domains (for example, switches or bridges, which are discussed later in this section).

Managed Hubs

Some hubs are equipped with the ability to capture statistics about network traffic and to accept control commands from a workstation on the network. Such *managed hubs* make it easier to troubleshoot and maintain a network.

Hub management software is often very closely tied to the hardware of the hub. It is therefore not unusual to find software that works with only one manufacturer's hubs. For example, if you were to purchase a hub, switching hub, or switch from Hewlett Packard's Advance Stack line, then you would be able to use the NetCenter software that the company provides.

The type of information and control a managed hub can provide for you usually includes the following:

♦ Viewing current status of the hub: As illustrated in Figure 5-4, the information provided to the user includes a measure of the utilization of the hub, the percentage of time taken up by collisions, the number of packets (frames) broadcast per second, and the percentage of errors detected in the frame check sequence (FCS).

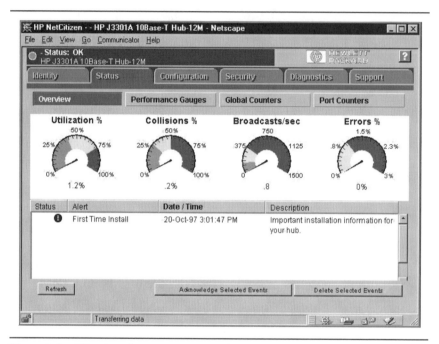

Figure 5-4:   Viewing the current status of a managed hub

♦ Viewing the status of a single port: As you can see in Figure 5-5, individual port statistics are the same as those for the entire hub.
♦ Configuring the hub: In Figure 5-6, for example, you can see that the software shows a replica of the managed hub and allows the user to use a mouse to activate and deactivate individual ports. In addition, the user can set IP

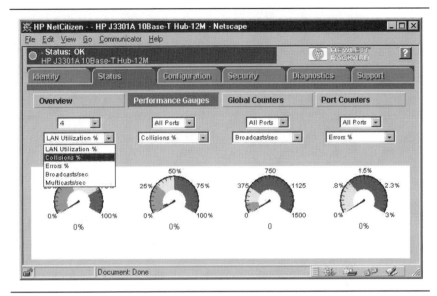

Figure 5-5:   Viewing the status of one port on a managed hub

addresses and choose what information is gathered about the system.

♦ Managing security

♦ Collecting hub and port usage statistics over time

Fast Ethernet Hub Considerations

If you look at the Fast Ethernet standard, you will discover that there are actually two types of Fast Ethernet hubs: Class I and Class II. The two classes differ in their electrical configurations and therefore have different benefits and limits on how they can be used.

Class I and Class II Hubs

Class I hubs cannot be cascaded. As a result, there can be only one Class I hub on a segment unless the hubs are *stackable*. (Stackable hubs are discussed a bit later in this section.) If there is more than one Class I hub on a network, then there must be a switch or router between the each Class I hub.

For practical purposes, this means that no more than one Class I hub can be in the network between any two network devices. For

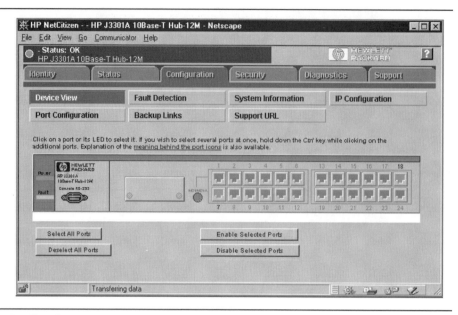

Figure 5-6: Configuring ports on a managed hub

example, the configuration in Figure 5-7(a) is fine because there is only one hub between network devices A and B. However, the configuration in Figure 5-7(b) will not work because several paths between devices include two Class I hubs (for example, A to C, A to D, B to C, and B to D).

> *Note: The labeling of the Class I hub with a Roman numeral in a circle comes from the Fast Ethernet standard.*

The benefit to a Class I hub is that it can handle more than one type of Ethernet media. For example, it might be able to accept both 10BASE-TX and 10BASE-T4 connections.

Class II hubs can be cascaded, but only two hubs deep. You can therefore have two Class I hubs on a segment. The only exception is if the hubs are stackable, in which case there can be at most two stacks on a segment.

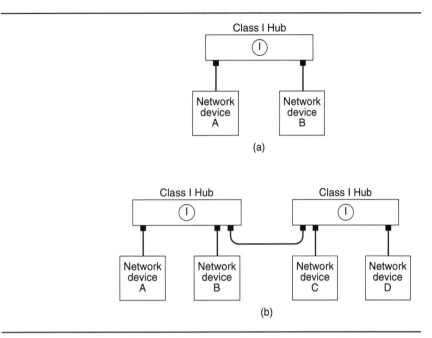

Figure 5-7: **(a) Acceptable Fast Ethernet configuration using a Class I hub (b) Unacceptable Fast Ethernet configuration using Class I hubs**

If you replace the Class I hubs in Figure 5-7 with Class II hubs, you can then place two hubs between any two network devices. (The maximum distance between the hubs is limited to 5 meters.) The configuration in Figure 5-8 is therefore acceptable. The drawback to a Class II hub, however, is that it is limited to a single type of media.

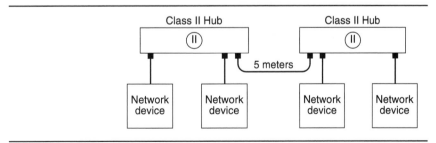

Figure 5-8: **Acceptable Fast Ethernet configuration using Class II hubs**

Given that most Fast Ethernet networks today are based on Category 5 UTP wire, the limitation to a single type of media is usually not significant.

There is one additional limitation to Class I and Class II hubs of which you should be aware: You cannot connect a Class I hub directly to a Class II hub; there must be a switch or router between them.

Stackable Hubs

One way to get around the limitations of Class I and Class II hubs is use *stackable hubs* such as those in Figure 5-9. Stackable hubs are designed not only to sit one on top of another, but they connect together with special stacking cables. The entire stack of hubs then looks to the network as if it were one hub. This is a simple and workable solution as long as no single network device is more than 100 meters from the hubs.

Figure 5-9:   Fast Ethernet stackable hubs (courtesy of 3Com Corporation)

The other major limitation to both standard and Fast Ethernet configurations is something known as *propagation delay*, the time it takes for a signal to be broadcast and read by all devices on a network. As a network grows large, cable distances may become so long that a device may not be able to finish transmitting before it has a chance to detect collisions from other transmissions. Propagation delay is the major reason for the cable length limits on standard Ethernet installations.

To prevent this on a Fast Ethernet network, you must take overall cable distances into account when planning the network layout. You start with a table of the average round-trip delays, expressed in *bit times,* for the devices on your network (see Table 5-1). Since the maximum allowable bit times between any two devices is 512, you add up the delays between the two devices on the network that are the farthest apart from one another. If the result is less than 512, then the network configuration will work.

Type of hardware	Delay per meter	Maximum delay
Two 100BASE-TX or 100BASE-FX devices		100
Two 100BASE-T4 devices		138
One 100BASE-TX or 100BASE-FX device and one 100BASE-T4 device		127
Category 3 cable segment	1.14	114/100 meters
Category 4 cable segment	1.14	114/100 meters
Category 5 cable segment	1.112	111.2/100 meters
Fiber optic cable	1.00	412/412 meters
Class I hub		140
Class I hub (all ports TX or FX)		92
Class II hub (any port T4)		67

Table 5-1: Sample Fast Ethernet round-trip propagation delays, expressed in bit times

As an example, consider again the network in Figure 5-8. Assume that all devices are 100BASE-TX and that the network uses the following lengths of Category 5 UTP wire:

♦ Network device A to hub: 100 meters
♦ Network device B to hub: 50 meters

♦ First hub to second hub: 5 meters
♦ Network device C to hub: 25 meters
♦ Network device D to hub: 50 meters

The longest path through the network is therefore from device A to device D, through the two hubs. We can therefore calculate the propagation delay for a signal to travel that path as follows:

```
Network device A = 100 bit times
Network device D = 100 bit times
First hub = 92 bit times
Second hub = 92 bit times
Cable from device A to hub = 100 * 1.112 = 111.2 bit times
Cable from first to second hub = 5 * 1.112 = 5.56 bit times
Cable from device D to hub = 50 * 1.112 = 55.6 bit times

Total bit times = 556.36 bit times
```

Since the result is greater than the maximum of 512, this is not an acceptable network configuration. However, if we shorten the cable length between device A and its hub to 50 meters, then the network will work.

```
Network device A = 100 bit times
Network device D = 100 bit times
First hub = 92 bit times
Second hub = 92 bit times
Cable from device A to hub = 50 * 1.112 = 55.6 bit times
Cable from first to second hub = 5 * 1.112 = 5.56 bit times
Cable from device D to hub = 50 * 1.112 = 55.6 bit times

Total bit times = 500.76 bit times
```

Multispeed Hubs

Many of the Ethernet hubs and NICs available today can handle both 10 Mbps and 100 Mbps UTP connections. To manage devices communicating at different speeds, such hardware uses *auto-negotiation*, a process during which a hub and a NIC exchange information about the highest speed each can handle. Transmission will then use that highest-possible speed.

Auto-negotiation is most effective if all devices in the network are equipped with auto-negotiation capabilities. However, a network may contain some NICs that do not have that ability. In that case, an auto-negotiating hub will recognize that the device is unable to respond to auto-negotiation signals. The hub will then determine what type of transmission the device can provide and, if the hub can handle that type of transmission, will switch to it. This makes it possible to take existing 10BASE-T devices and include them on a network with 100BASE-TX and/or 100BASE-T4 devices using a single multispeed hub.

For the easiest integration of 10 Mbps and 100 Mbps devices on the same network, look for a mention of auto-negotiation in the literature that describes hubs and NICs. Fortunately, most 10/100 equipment currently being sold does perform auto-negotiations.

Bridges (Switches) and Switching Hubs

The hubs that we have been discussing to this point create a single, large collision domain. As you have been reading, there are some significant limitations in terms of distance and number of network devices placed on such configurations. If you need to add more devices or cover more distance than a single collision domain will support, then you will need to connect individual network segments with some type of hardware that creates a network with multiple collision domains. The most commonly used devices to do so are *bridges* (also simply called *switches*) and *switching hubs* (for an example, see Figure 5-10).

> Note: If you read data communications textbooks, you will find a clear-cut difference between bridges and switching hubs. However, in practice most manufacturers seem to call everything a "switch." This means that you must read vendor literature closely to be certain of what you are purchasing.

If you can't find a preconfigured switch that has the right type and number of ports for your needs, you can also puchase an empty chassis into which you insert interface modules. For example, the 7-slot chassis in Figure 5-11 has been filled with 10BASE-T modules

Figure 5-10:   A switch (coutesy of 3Com Corporation)

(the RJ-11 jacks in the bottom five slots) and a pair of fiber optic connectors in the sixth slot from the bottom. The chassis also provides three connectors for integrating the switch into a network.

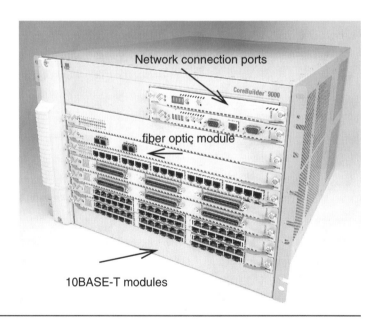

Figure 5-11:   A 7-slot chassis filled with switch modules (courtesy of 3Com Corporation)

Bridges, with only two ports, were the first devices to connect independent collision domains. Switching hubs can handle more than two ports and are therefore a bit more complex. For simplicity's sake, we will call all of these devices switches.

Switches operate in Layer 2 of the TCP/IP protocol stack (the Data Link layer). This is in contrast to hubs, which operate in the Physical layer.

Switch Learning

One of the most important benefits of using a switch is that the switch can learn the configuration of the network itself. Assume, for example, that you have the simple connections that appear in Figure 5-12, where three unmanaged hubs are connected to a switch. Those devices connected to hub A represent one collision domain; those connected to hub B represent a second collision domain; the device connected to hub C represents yet a third.

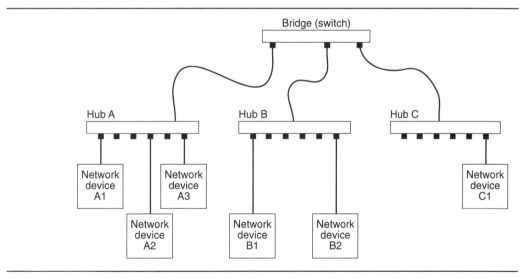

Figure 5-12:   Connecting three collision domains with a switch

When you first power up the switch, it has no idea what is connected to its ports. However, as packets move through the network, the switch builds a table of which devices are where and uses that table to route packets to their destination, rather than broadcasting every packet to every connected device as a hub would do.

For example, the first time device A1 sends a packet to device B1, the switch learns that hub A and device A1 are connected to a particular port. Since it does not know where the destination device is connected, it broadcasts the packet to every port with the exception of the port through which the packet arrived (to hubs B and C). When device B1 responds to A1's transmission, the switch learns the location of hub B and device B1.

Suppose a packet leaves devices A2, destined for device A1. The switch knows that A1 is connected to hub A. Once it realizes that A2 is also connected to hub A, it knows that it can ignore the packet. A1 was able to read the packet from the bus inside hub A.

The next time a packet moves from A1 to B1, the switch knows exactly where B1 is located. Rather than broadcasting the packet to every port, it sends the packet directly to the port to which hub B is connected.

This method of learning works very well as long as the devices on the network do not change. However, over time devices are powered up and down, making the table of locations that the switch has assembled obsolete.

The solution is actually simpler than you might think. Every few minutes, the switch erases its table and starts over. Because there are so many packets traveling between stations, the learning process is actually very fast and it does not take the switch long to recreate an accurate location table.

> *Note: Although the switches we have been considering have connected multiple Ethernet segments, it is possible to find switches that bridge network segments using different MAC protocols. Multiprotocol switches are most often used to connect Ethernet and Token Ring segments into a single network. Such hardware tends to be relatively expensive because the*

switch must disassemble the packet used by one protocol and re-
assemble it into the packet format of the other protocol before
sending the packet on its way.

Looping Problems

In theory, switches must be connected in such a way that they do
not contain any loops. If a loop does occur, as in Figure 5-13, traffic
may endlessly travel around the network, never reaching its destination.

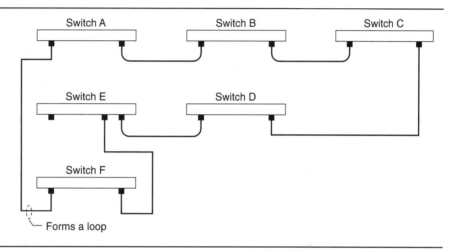

Figure 5-13:   A switched network containing a loop

The problem occurs because the loop introduces more than one path
to a given network address. Assume, for example, that switch A in
Figure 5-13 needs to send a packet to a device connected through
switch D. Depending on how switch A learned to find switch D, the
path may be A–B–C–D or A–E–D. Switch B must also learn the path
to switch D, which could be either B–C–D or B–A–E–D.

For this example, assume that switch A is using an A–B–C–D path.
However, when the packet reaches switch B, switch B uses the B–A–
E–D path and sends the packet right back to switch A. The two
switches will then endlessly exchange the same packet. As more
packets get caught in this type of loop, the network will bog down
with packets that are never delivered.

There are two solutions to this problem. The first is to ensure that a network never contains any loops. In a relatively small network, this is not terribly difficult. However, as networks grow, it can be hard to keep track of exactly how network segments are connected and therefore where a loop might occur. In that case, you need switches that implement a *spanning-tree algorithm*, a method for ensuring that there is only one path from one switch to another in a network.

A group of switches in the same "tree" select one switch as the "root" of the tree. (This is usually the switch with the lowest Ethernet address.) Then, the root collects configuration information from all the switches in the tree and sends that information to every switch involved. Each switch then computes a single path from its own location to the root, therefore ensuring that there is no more than one path between any two switches.

> *Note: To make it easy to communicate with all the switches in the tree, the root switch uses a multicast address, an address that is recognized by a group of devices on a network. In fact, a broadcast (a packet sent to all ports) is simply a multicast address that is recognized by all devices connected to the switch.*

Switch Limitations

Switches are well suited to small and medium-size networks. However, there are some limitations to their configuration and use, including the following:

- There should be no more than seven switches in the route from one network device to another to avoid unacceptable transmission delays.
- Switches cannot optimize the routing between themselves. The routes that packets travel from one switch to another depend on the order in which transmissions occurred during the route-learning process and are unrelated to what might be the shortest path between two switches.
- Switched networks are not especially fault-tolerant. In particular, switches (even those that support the spanning-tree

algorithm) cannot provide alternatives routes to work around a switch or transmission line that may be down.

Switches are also considerably more expensive than hubs. For example, at the time this book was written unmanaged 10BASE-T hubs cost between $6 and $12 per port; 10/100BASE-T unmanaged hubs cost just under $40 per port. In contrast, 10BASE-T switches were running around $80 per port, while 10/100BASE-T switches cost between $100 and $175 per port. (As with all computer hardware, these prices are bound to come down, but they serve as indicators of relative costs.)

Routers

If your network is too large to be built from switches or if it needs more sophisticated routing capabilities, then you will probably need to turn to a *router*, a piece of hardware that works in Layer 3 of the OSI and TCP/IP protocol stacks (the Network layer). A router not only provides switching functions, but can optimize routes, steer packets around failed connections, and manage sharing of connections to the Internet (either through a modem or a dedicated line).

TCP/IP Router Addressing

Because routers work at the Network Layer, rather than the physical layer, they need a way of addressing network devices that is independent of physical placement. Assuming that your network is using TCP/IP, the addresses will be *IP* (*Internet Protocol*) *numbers*. Each network device must have its own unique IP number.

Assigning IP Addresses

IP numbers are in the format X.X.X.X, where each X is a value between 0 and 255 (a byte). The first one, two, or three Xs represent the *network part* of the address because they identify an entire network. The number of bytes used as the network part of an IP address indicates the class of the network and limits both the number of unique networks allowed in that class and the number of nodes supported per network. In Table 5-2, you can see the three classes of networks currently in use.

Address class	Address range	Bytes in network part	Number of networks in the class	Number of nodes per network
A	0.0.0.0[a] to 127.255.255.255	1	126[b]	>16 million
B	128.0.0.0 to 191.255.255.255	2	16,384	65,534
C	192.0.0.0 to 223.255.255.255	3	2,097,152	254

Table 5-2:   IP address classes

[a]   0.0.0.0 cannot be assigned to a network; it is used as a broadcast address to refer to all nodes on the current network.

[b]   There are only 126 (rather 128) addresses in class A because 0.0.0.0 is reserved as the broadcast address and 127.0.0.0 is reserved as a loopback address to enable nodes to communicate with themselves.

Note: Class D addresses (224.0.0.0 to 239.255.255.255) are reserved for multicasting. Class E addresses (240.0.0.0 to 247.255.255.255) are reserved for future use.

For example, the author's network uses 205.1.1 as the network part of its address, which means it is a class C network. You can figure out the class of an address by checking the range of the first byte.

The remaining numbers uniquely identify a specific network device (the *host part*). In the author's network, 205.1.1.1 is the main publishing workstation, 205.1.1.2 is the database server, 205.1.1.3 is the fax server, 205.1.1.4 is a connection for a laptop (either Windows 95 or Macintosh OS), 205.1.1.5 is a Windows 95 computer, 205.1.1.6 is the printer, 205.1.1.7 is the Linux server, and 205.1.1.8 is a remote database client computer connected through a pair of wireless bridges. (For more details about wireless computing in very small networks, see Appendix A.)

Note: The idea originally behind the IP addressing scheme was that there would be a very few networks with a large number of nodes and many more smaller networks. The 2,113,662 net-

works provided for in this 32-bit addressing scheme, however, are quickly being used up by the proliferation of corporate networks. There is, however, a proposal — IPv6 — that provides for a 128-bit IP address. These new addresses are slowly being phased in as needed. Fortunately, the current 32-bit addresses will remain valid, so that existing networks do not have to be changed.

If your network is never going to be connected directly to the Internet, then you can make up IP addresses for all your equipment, using any address class you want. However, if you think that there is even the remotest chance that you will be providing a direct Internet connection at any time in the future, then you should use the IP address ranges reserved for private internets. You can find those ranges in Table 5-3.

Network class	Address range
A	10.0.0.0 to 10.255.255.255
B	172.16.0.0 to 172.31.255.255
C	192.168.0.0 to 192.168.255.255

Table 5-3:   IP address spaces for private internets

When a network is connected directly to the Internet, the IP addresses of all nodes must be unique within the entire Internet. Ultimate responsibility for assigning IP numbers rests with the Internet Assigned Numbers Authority (IANA). However, numbers are actually assigned by regional registries. In the United States, for example, registration is handled by the American Registry for Internet Numbers (ARIN). IP numbers are assigned in large blocks, usually to Internet service providers (ISPs). In most cases, you will therefore get the network part of your IP numbers from whatever ISP will be providing your connection to the Internet.

Note: You can reach ARIN at http://www.arin.net.

Note: For in-depth information about Internet addressing, see
TCP/IP Addressing by Graham, published by AP Professional.

Routers must also have IP numbers, one for each network to which
they are connected. For example, the router in Figure 5-14(a) (a *dual-
homed* router because it is connected to two networks), needs two IP
numbers so that it can distinguish between the switches that are
connected to it.

In Figure 5-14(b), the routers are *multihomed* because they connect to
more than two networks each. Router A, for example, is connected
to a switch, to the Internet, and to the network that runs between
the three routers. Routers B and C are connect to the other inter-
router network and to two switches each. This means that each of
these routers will be working with three IP numbers, one for each
network to which it is connected.

Addressing Subnets

As you have been reading throughout this chapter, large networks
are generally broken up into segments (*subnets*) that are connected
by hardware such as routers. In that case, a portion of the IP address
is used to identify the subnet to which a device is connected.

Class A and B networks use the third portion of the IP address to
indicate the subnet. For example, if a network device has an address
of 172.17.2.3 and the network is divided into subnets, the device is
number 3 on subnet number 2 on network 172.17. This scheme provides for up to 254 subnets, each with up to 254 devices. (The addresses X.X.0.0 and X.255.255.255 are not available for assignment
to network devices; they are used as broadcast addresses.)

Subnetting a class C network is a bit trickier. (The original develop-
ers of the IP addressing scheme did not think that class C networks
would ever need to be subnetted, although doing so is not uncom-
mon today.) The third byte of the IP address is used to identify the
network, so some of the host part must be allocated to the subnet.
For example, you could use the first two bits of the host part to indicate the subnet, providing you with two subnets with up to 62 devices each. Allocating three bits to the subnet would give you a

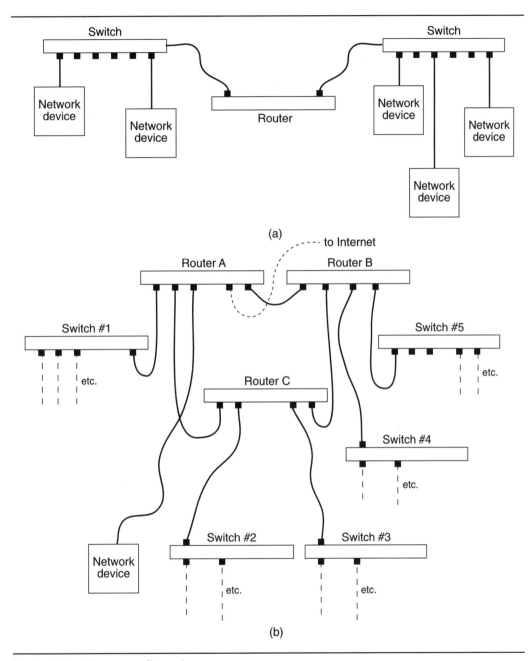

Figure 5-14: **Router configurations**

possible six subnets with up to 30 devices each. (Again, remember that bit patterns of all 0s or all 1s are not valid IP addresses for network devices, reducing the number of possible subnets/devices by two.)

When you configure a TCP/IP configuration for a network device, you will see space for a *subnet mask*. This is a pattern of bits that masks out the host part of the address. For example, the typical class B subnet mask is 255.255.255.0. If you perform a logical AND with this mask and an IP address, you will get all 0s in the host part, isolating the network and subnet portions of the address only.

TCP/IP Router Operations

When TCP/IP is used to route a network packet (called a *datagram* in TCP/IP terminology), both the transmitting system and the router may be involved in sending the packet. The process works something like this:

♦ The transmitting system examines the IP address of the message. If the network part of the receiver's address is the same as the transmitter's address (the two devices are on the same network), then the transmitter sends the packet directly to the receiver, without involving a router. This situation would occur if a device connected to Switch #4 in Figure 5-14(b) were sending a message to any other device connected to that same switch.

♦ If the IP address indicates that the message is to go to a device on a different network, the transmitting system sends the packet to its default router (the router it has been configured to use unless that router is unavailable). For example, in Figure 5-14(b), this occurs when a device on Switch #4 needs to send a message to a device on Switch #5.

♦ The router examines the IP address of the message. If the message goes to a network connected directly to the router, the router sends the packet on its way, as it would when transferring a message from a device on Switch #4 to a device on Switch #5. However, if the message is destined for a device on a network that is not connected to the router, the router sends the packet to the "next" router in the path to the destination. For example, if a device on Switch #4 needs to send a message to a device on Switch #1, Router B will send the packet to Router A, which in turn will route the packet to Switch #1.

IPX/SPX Router Addressing and Operation

Addressing using the IPX/SPX protocol stack is much simpler than TCP/IP, primarily because networks using IPX/SPX are self-contained; they are not connected to an ever-changing global network. Each network segment is identified by a unique *network address* that is assigned when a network operating system using the protocols is installed on a server. (The size and format of the network address depends on the NOS.) This address needs to be unique only within the network.

The network devices are then differentiated by the unique physical addresses assigned to their NICs by the NIC manufacturers. The destination address of an IPX/SPX packet therefore has two components: the logical network address of a network segment and the physical address of the device on that segment.

When a router receives a packet transmitted by IPX/SPX, it first checks the network address to determine the network segment to which the packet is to be sent. The packet is then routed to the router to which to network segment is connected. That router checks the physical address in the packet to determine the precise device to which the packet should be sent.

VINES Router Addressing and Operation

VINES, the proprietary protocol stack developed for use with the Banyan VINES network operating system, uses yet another way of addressing network devices. Like IPX/SPX, VINES does not connect directly to a global network and therefore only requires that its addresses be unique within the network.

Note: for additional information about the VINES protocol stack and the Banyan VINES NOS, see Chapter 8.

Each node is given a 48-bit address made up of a four-byte network number and a two-byte subnetwork number. The network number is determined by a physical key (a *dongle*) attached to the parallel port on the NOS server. The server's subnet number is always 0001. Subnet numbers for other devices are assigned dynamically by a routing server when the devices are powered up and join the network.

A device joining the network sends a broadcast to all of the servers on the same physical media as itself. One of the servers responds with its own network number and the next available subnet number. The server that responds becomes the routing server for the device until the device is powered down and leaves the network.

Note: If a network device's routing server goes down, you must reboot the device so that it will be able to contact another server and get a new subnet number.

Network addresses are bound to device names by an application called StreetTalk. These names, in the format item@group@organization, make it easier for users to specify the destinations of messages they send.

Each routing server maintains two routing tables: a Known Networks table and a Neighbors table. The Known Networks table contains the following:

- ♦ The location of known networks, regardless of whether they are local or remote.
- ♦ The location of the nearest "next" network.
- ♦ The relative "cost" of reaching each known network in terms of the round-trip delay, measured in increments of 200 ms.
- ♦ An idle timer. (Servers that are idle for 96 hours or more are dropped from the routing table.)

The Neighbors table contains the following:

- The location of every other server connected to the same physical media.
- The location of every device to which the server has assigned a subnet number.
- The location of every device with which the server is communicating directly.

Network devices also maintain Known Networks and Neighbors tables. A device's Known Networks table contains information about only those networks with which it is communicating. A device's Neighbors table has information about the device's routing server and any other devices with which it is communicating directly.

A router handling VINES protocols uses a fairly straightforward process to decide what to do with an incoming packet.

- If the packet is addressed to the server, the packet is handled without further transmission.
- If the packet is a broadcast packet, the router checks the destination address of the packet. If the router is on the least-cost path to the destination, then it resends the packet through all of its ports except the one from which the packet came. The router also processes the packet for its own use. Otherwise, it discards the packet.
- If the packet is addressed to another device, the router checks to see if the destination is a neighbor. If so, the packet is sent directly to the neighbor. If not, the packet is sent to the next router on the least-cost path to the destination.

AppleTalk Router Addressing and Operation

Like IPX/SPX, AppleTalk networks are self-contained and do not need to worry about addresses that are globally unique. AppleTalk addresses only need to be unique within the network.

An AppleTalk address is made up of three parts:

- The *socket number*: Identifies a network connection on a network device. Any given piece of equipment can have one or more sockets. For example, most of today's Macintoshes have LocalTalk and 10BASE-T Ethernet ports, each of which represents a separate socket. The socket number is a physical address assigned by the hardware manufacturer.
- The *node ID*: A number that uniquely identifies the network device. Each device chooses a node ID when it is powered up. Macintoshes remember their last-used node ID in battery-maintained PRAM (parameter RAM), but other devices must choose a new ID each time they join the network. To choose a node ID, a device begins with 0 and then checks the network segment to see if there is another device with the same node ID. If there is, the device tries the next highest ID and checks again. It continues the process until it finds an unused ID. The benefit of this process is that a device can be moved from one network segment to another without needing any address reconfiguration.
- The *network number*: A number that uniquely identifies the network segment, which is known as a *zone*.

To handle AppleTalk traffic, a router first checks the network number and sends the packet to the router identified by that number. The second router then sends the packet to the correct node ID and socket.

Router Benefits and Drawbacks

The biggest drawback to a router is that it represents an additional hardware cost beyond that of whatever hubs and/or switches your network may already be using. However, by investing the extra money in the router, you gain the following:

- You can create larger networks using routers than you can with switches alone. Remember that in a switched network there can be no more than seven devices, including switches, in the path between any two network devices. A router gets you around the seven-hop limit.

♦ Routers are designed to handle connections between networks using different protocols.

♦ Routers can optimize the path between any two network devices (in particular, to balance the load on the network) and can reroute packets to travel around unavailable devices.

♦ Routers make it possible for many computers to share a single high-speed connection to the Internet, such as an ISDN or T1 line. Alternatively, routers may contain multiple modems, each connected to a separate POTS line. The router then assigns computers to modems as requests for dial-out connections arrive at the router.

Structured Cabling Systems

To this point, we have talked about the pieces of hardware that go together to make up an Ethernet network. A well-designed network, however, is more than just cables and hubs and switches and routers and computers strung together haphazardly. For ease of maintenance and expansion, the layout of a network needs to be planned.

Two standards-making bodies—the Electronic Industries Association/Telecommunications Industry Association (EIA/TIA) and the International Standards Organization (ISO)—have issued standards for the wiring of commercial buildings for data and telecommunications (*structured cabling systems*). Both sets of standards are very similar. Therefore, for this discussion we will be focusing on the EIA/TIA 568-A standard, which is the most commonly used. The goal of that standard is to describe a building wiring system that has a usable life of more than 10 years.

The design of a structured cabling system should be independent of any specific vendor's equipment. It should also encompass the entire building so that equipment can be moved around as needed and reconnected without requiring any wiring changes.

Parts of a Structured Cabling System

There are six major parts to a 568-A structured cabling system:

- *Work area*: The location of one or more devices that are connected to the network. The work area includes the network devices and the cables that connect them to a network outlet in the wall.
- *Horizontal cabling*: Runs from network jacks in the wall to hubs, switches, and routers, wherever they might be located. For the most part, horizontal cabling is limited to a single floor and hidden within walls.
- *Telecommunications closet* (also known as a *wiring closet*): A cabinet on a floor of a building that houses hubs, switches, and/or routers or the equivalent wiring. Horizontal cabling connects network wall jacks to telecommunications closets. Backbone cabling connects telecommunications closets into a single network.
- *Backbone cabling*: Cabling that provides an interconnection between major network segments, in particular, between the floors of a building. For example, in Figure 5-14, the network created by the cabling between the routers might be considered a backbone, especially if the routers are on different floors of a building.
- *Equipment room*: A more complex telecommunications closet, where building- or location-wide equipment is installed.
- *Entrance facility*: The connection between the network in a building and the outside world. This may include connections to the Internet, to telephone service, or to networks in other buildings.

The relationship of all these elements is diagrammed in Figure 5-15.

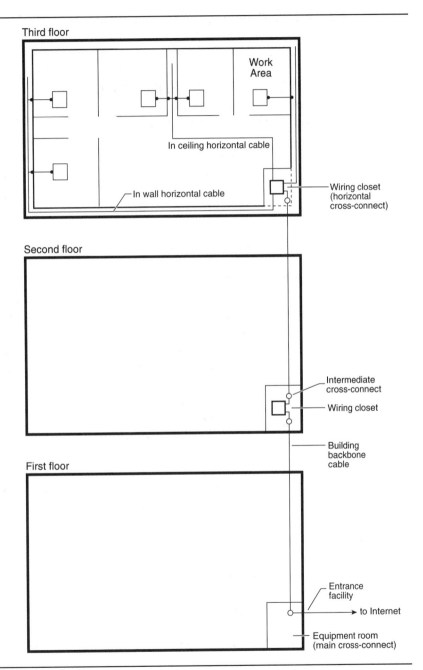

Figure 5-15:   Parts of a structured cabling system

Work Area Facilities

Because structured cabling systems include telephone service as well as computer networking, they require two outlets in each work area. The first outlet should accept 4-pair 100 ohm UTP. The second should accept either 100 ohm UTP, 2-pair 150 ohm STP (*shielded twisted pair*), or two-fiber 62.5/125 μm multimode fiber. Typical installations include one Category 3 4-pair wire for voice communications and one Category 5 4-pair wire for data communications.

Equipment in a work area connects to the wall outlets with *patch cables*. These are generally short cables (6–12 feet) with either RJ-11 or RJ-45 jacks on either end.

Horizontal Cabling Guidelines

There are several guidelines in the structured cabling standards that apply to horizontal cabling.

- Horizontal cables run from wall outlets to wiring closets.
- Horizontal cables must be configured in the wiring closet in a star topology. For Ethernet, this means that the wiring closet must either contain hubs, switches, and/or routers or have wiring that provides the same type of function. In particular, the wiring closet may contain a *patch panel* into which UTP cables terminated with RJ-45 jacks can be plugged. In that case, the bus is the wiring that connects the jacks in the patch panel. Unlike a hub or other powered devices, the patch panel does not amplify and retransmit the signal. It simply provides the bus wiring on which the signal can travel. The wiring in a wiring closet is known as a *horizontal cross-connect* (HC).
- The wiring closet connects to an *intermediate cross-connect* (IC), the place at which the building backbone reaches the floor, or directly to the building backbone, which in turn is connected to the equipment room (the *main cross-connect* (MC).

♦ The maximum distance for any single piece of cable is 90 meters.

Note: In very large buildings, the maximum cable length of 90 meters may mean that a single floor requires more than one wiring closet. The wiring closets on that floor can then be connected with backbone cable, which in turn are connected to the building backbone.

♦ Copper-based wiring must not be bridged or spliced, although fiber optic cable can be spliced.

Category 5 4-pair 100 ohm UTP is recommended for horizontal cabling. However, 230 ohm STP and 50/125 μm multimode optical fiber are also acceptable.

Outlet Wiring

The EIA/TIA 568 standard includes two schemes for wiring modular outlets in walls. As you can see in Figure 5-16, the wiring in the T568A is the same as the wiring in the T568B standard except that pairs 2 and 3 are reversed. Either type of wiring can be used for both ISDN connections and for 10BASE-T and 100BASE-T networking.

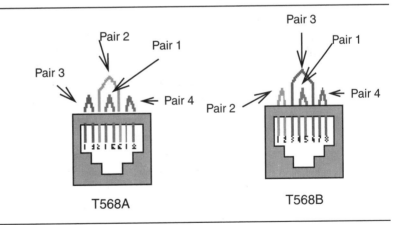

Figure 5-16: Outlet wiring standards (courtesy of The Siemon Company)

An alternative is to use the USOC wiring standards for wall outlets, which support jacks with 1-, 2-, 3-, or 4-pair wiring (see Figure 5-17). One advantage of the USOC wiring is that you use a 6-position jack in an 8-position outlet. However, this is not recommended by most vendors because the insertion and removal of the 6-position jack may damage the unused positions in the outlet.

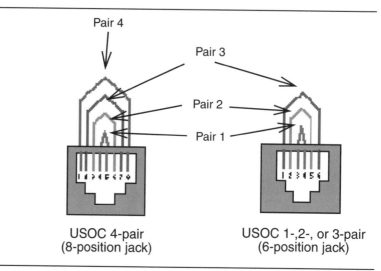

Pair 4

Pair 3

Pair 2

Pair 1

USOC 4-pair
(8-position jack)

USOC 1-,2-, or 3-pair
(6-position jack)

Figure 5-17:   USOC outlet wiring standards (courtesy of The Siemon Company)

UTP Cable Wiring

There are two main uses for patch cords in a structured cabling system. The first is to run cables between ports in a patch panel. The second is to connect network devices to wall outlets. The wiring of the cabling *may* be different for these two uses, depending on the wiring of wall outlets.

UTP patch cables that are used between patch panels are always wired *straight-through*. This means that the wiring is identical in each connector at the end of the cable. For example, pin 1 at one end is connected to pin 1 at the other, and so on.

UTP patch cables that are used to connect network devices to wall outlets may be wired straight-through or they may be reversed, producing a *crossover cable*. In a 10BASE-T cable, for example, pin 1 is connected to pin 6, pin 2 is connected to pin 3, pin 3 is connected to pin 2, and pin 6 is connected to pin 1. The effect is to take a transmitted signal and transfer it to the receive pins on the other end of the cable, and vice versa.

You will need to check with the manufacturers of your network devices and NICs to determine whether a straight-through or crossover cable is required to connect the device to a wall outlet. However, if you happen to run into an unlabeled cable, it is fairly easy to tell which of the two it is.

Put the connectors side by side, with the contacts facing you, as in Figure 5-18. The compare the colors of the wires from left to right. If the wire colors are exactly the same, then you have a straight-through cable. If the colors are reversed, you have a crossover cable.

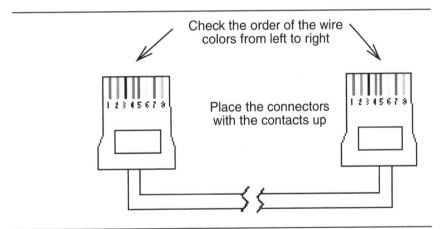

Figure 5-18: Checking the type of UTP cable wiring (courtesy of The Siemon Company)

Backbone Cabling Guidelines

Like horizontal cabling, there are a number of guidelines that relate to the design for backbone cabling.

♦ Backbone cabling in a structured cabling system is restricted to a star topology.
♦ Each horizontal cross-connect (represented by a wiring closet) is to be connected to only one intermediate cross-connect, which in turn is connected directly to the main cross-connect. Alternatively, a horizontal cross-connect can be connected directly to the main cross-connect.
♦ Backbone cabling can be constructed from 100 ohm UTP, 120 ohm UTP, 150 ohm STP, 62.5/125 μm multimode optical fiber, 50/125 μm multimode optical fiber, and single-mode optical fiber. Any of these types of cables can be used in combination as needed. If a backbone is made up of different types of cables, the connections for all those cables must still be in the same building.
♦ The lengths of individual cabling runs depend on the type of cable and what is being connected. A summary of cabling length guidelines for all structured cabling system can be found in Table 5-4.

Type of cable	Work area to HC	HC to IC	IC to MC	HC to MC
UTP for voice communications	90 meters	500 meters	300 meters	800 meters
Category 3 UTP ($\leq$ 16 MHz)	90 meters	90 meters	90 meters	90 meters
Category 5 UTP ($\leq$ 100 MHz)	90 meters	90 meters	90 meters	90 meters
STP ($\leq$ 300 ohm)	90 meters	90 meters	90 meters	90 meters
62.5 μm multimode optical fiber	90 meters	500 meters	1500 meters	2000 meters
Single-mode optical fiber	90 meters	500 meters	2500 meters	3000 meters

Table 5-4:   **Structured cabling lengths**

6

Integrating Wireless Transmissions

Businesses consider wireless networking for two main reasons:

- ◆ A wireless device, such as a hand-held computer or inventory counter, gives the user mobility. For example, an inventory taker can walk through a warehouse or store and still be in contact with the network. In this case, the wireless device is an extension of an existing wired network.
- ◆ Wireless transmitters can be used to replace wired connections, making it possible to dispense with the need to run cabling.

There are trade-offs in adding wireless connections to an Ethernet. Some wireless solutions require line-of-sight connections. They can therefore be used only within a single, open office space. However, such transmissions use a wide-angle, high-dispersion signal and may be intercepted by someone with a passive receiver. Wireless transmissions that go through walls and floors alleviate the line-of-sight requirement but are more susceptible to security breaches because an unauthorized receiver of the transmission is less easily noticed. Some wireless vendors therefore encrypt the signals while they are in the air.

Wireless transmissions are generally slower than wired transmissions, working at speeds of 1 Mbps to 10 Mbps. At the time this book was written, there were no Fast Ethernet wireless solutions.

> *Note: When you are constructing a wired network, you can combine equipment from multiple vendors without a problem because network standards ensure interoperability. However, current wireless standards only govern the MAC protocol to be used by wireless Ethernet, making wireless solutions more proprietary than are wired solutions. Typically, when you commit to a wireless network, you are also committing to a vendor. That is why this chapter is far more vendor-specific than anything you have encountered so far.*

Using Wireless Devices to Extend a Wired Network

One of the most common uses of wireless technology is to provide mobility for users. For example, you might want inventory takers or warehouse workers using hand-held devices to send their input directly to your network. Or you might want laptop users to be able to move around the building and still remain connected to the network.

A wireless solution for mobile users means that signals must travel from the mobile device to some type of receiver connected to the wired network. Typically, this requires signals to travel through walls and floors. Therefore, the signal type of choice is a radio signal (or RF, for radio frequency).

RF wireless networks use a variation on the Ethernet MAC protocol known as *Carrier Sense Multiple Access with Collision Avoidance* (CS-MA/CA). This means that devices on the network do not detect collisions, as do true Ethernet devices. Instead, a device checks to see if the network is idle—it looks to see if there is a carrier—and if idle, transmits a packet. The device avoids collisions because it does not transmit when the network is in use.

Connection Hardware

One typical architecture is that provided by RangeLAN2 (Proxim, Inc.). Each remote device is equipped with either a transceiver such as the PC card for laptops in Figure 6-1 or the ISA card for desktops in Figure 6-2; or it is connected to an Ethernet adapter such as that in Figure 6-3. Notice that the adapter has a single 10BASE-T port. It can therefore be connected to either a single device or to an entire 10BASE-T segment.

Figure 6-1: A RangeLAN2 PC card with transceiver (courtesy of Proxim, Inc.)

The Ethernet adapter or the transceiver in the remote device serves as a connection between the devices connected to it and an access point (see Figure 6-4), which is then connected to the wired portion of the network.

As you can see in Figure 6-5, the access point connects directly to the wired network. It can then communicate with any devices or

Figure 6-2:   A RangeLAN2 ISA card with transceiver (courtesy of Proxim, Inc.)

Figure 6-3:   A RangeLAN2 Ethernet adapter (courtesy of Proxim, Inc.)

network segments equipped with transceivers. The remote devices therefore have access to the wired portion of the network, just as if they were wired as well.

Each RangeLAN2 transceiver has a maximum range of about 500 meters, although the actual range depends on the type of building materials used in the walls and floors through which the signal must pass. To extend the range, you can add additional access points and use them as extension points. A transmission then

Figure 6-4: A RangeLAN2 access/extension point (courtesy of Proxim, Inc.)

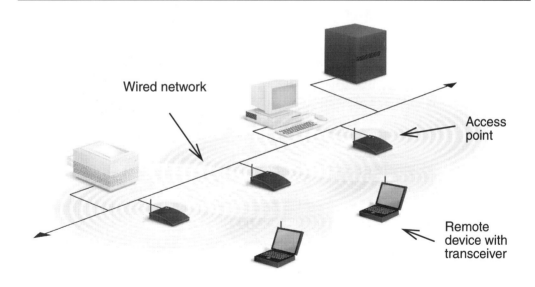

Figure 6-5: A sample topology for a wired network with wireless remote extensions (courtesy of Proxim, Inc.)

makes several hops from one extension point to another to reach the access point that is connected to the network.

Speed

The major drawback to using wireless transmissions, even for remote users, is speed. RangeLAN2, for example, transmits only at 1.6 Mbps, much slower than the 10 Mbps or 100 Mbps that a typical Ethernet can achieve.

Security

As mentioned earlier in this chapter, RF signals are relatively easy to intercept, especially since they can be intercepted without the transmitter or receiver realizing that the interception is occurring. All that is required is a receiver tuned to the same frequency that the wireless network is using.

To make such signal interception extremely difficult, wireless LANs use *frequency-hopping*, a technique where the specific frequency used for transmission varies rapidly. This makes it virtually impossible to tune a receiver to intercept enough of a transmission to be useful.

A number of wireless vendors also offer an encryption option, using DES, the Data Encryption Standard. DES makes a signal unintelligible to the relatively casual signal tapper. However, it can slow down the processing of data because it must be encrypted before it is sent over the network and decrypted when it is received. In addition, a determined signal stealer with significant computing power can crack DES codes.

> *Note: There is no foolproof encryption scheme today. The Beowolf supercomputers — supercomputers made up of a collection of PCs wired together — are relatively inexpensive and have the power to crack even the toughest encryption with several days of continuous processing. You can never be 100 percent secure.*

Therefore, you put in place as much security as you can afford, weighing the cost of a security breach against the likelihood of that breach. At some point, the risk of a breach is so low that it is not worth the cost of added security.

Using Wireless Transmission to Replace Wire

There are very few true wireless solutions that can be used to replace most wired connections. One specific example is FiRLAN, which uses infrared (IR) signals, the same type of signal used in most remote controls. FiRLAN uses the CSMD/CD protocol, which means that its components integrate easily into an existing wired Ethernet. Signals travel at 10 Mbps, the same speed as standard Ethernet.

Because FiRLAN uses an IR signal, it requires line-of-sight transmissions. Each network device, or group of devices, that is to be connected to the wireless portion of the network is connected to a FiRLAN transceiver such as that in Figure 6-6. The transceiver is either hung from the ceiling or placed on the top of an office cubicle wall. Each transceiver can handle up to 29 10BASE2 devices, or, with the addition of a concentrator, more than 8 10BASE-T devices.

Figure 6-6:   A FiRLAN transceiver (courtesy of A. T. Schindler Communications Inc.)

The range of the transceivers varies from 34 meters to 1500 meters, depending on the model. If an office needs longer distances, then a signal can be sent from one transceiver to another (a *multihop* transmission).

The signal is transmitted to a FiRLAN hub (see Figure 6-7), which in turn can be connected to a building backbone cable. A single hub can manage signals from up to 255 transceivers and can handle up to 29 direct network device connections, making it possible to cover an area of roughly 30,000 square feet with a single FiRLAN network.

A sample network configuration can be found in Figure 6-8. (The ET devices in the illustration are transceivers.) Keep in mind, however, that the line-of-sight requirement means that a FiRLAN network is generally restricted to a single floor.

Figure 6-7:   A FiRLAN hub (courtesy of A. T. Schindler Communications Inc.)

However, through the use of outdoor transceivers on the roofs or outside walls of buildings, FiRLAN can also be used to send signals from one building to another, assuming there is a direct line-of-sight between the transceivers. The IR signal will also pass through windows, so building-to-building transmissions can be established with indoor transceivers if the two windows line up.

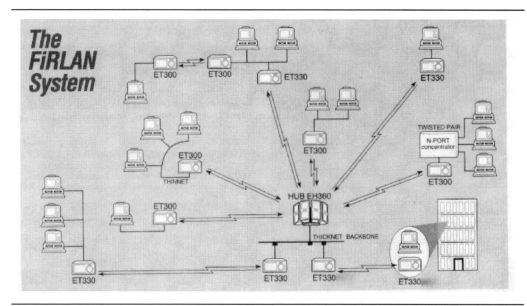

Figure 6-8: **Sample layout of a FiRLAN wireless network (courtesy of A. T. Schindler Communications Inc.)**

Outdoor transmissions are slightly susceptible to weather disruptions. During heavy snow or extremely foggy conditions, you may have to increase the range (in other words, the strength) of the signal to compensate for the loss caused by the weather.

When a FiRLAN hub receives a transmission, it repeats the signal to all attached transceivers. It therefore functions just like a wired Ethernet hub, broadcasting every signal to all attached devices.

In terms of a cost, a wireless solution such as FiRLAN is more expensive then a wired solution if you look simply at hub and transceiver prices. Why, then, would you bother to install it? There are several situations in which wiring does not make good sense:

  ♦ You are leasing a large office space that you have broken up into cubicles. The space does not belong to you and you do not know how long you will be using it. Therefore, you do not want to spend the money on wiring. A

wireless network like FiRLAN provides something you
can take with you, wherever your offices end up.

♦ Your company is growing and changing very rapidly.
You are constantly moving office partitions. It is therefore
more costly (and disruptive) to continually rewire for
new office configurations than it is to invest in a wireless
solution with transceivers that can be easily repositioned
as the office layout changes.

♦ The network environment includes a great deal of electrical or magnetic interference, extreme heat, or corrosive
chemicals that would negatively affect wiring.

♦ You often need to set up temporary networks at trade-
shows, client sites, schools, sporting events, disaster
sites, and so on. A wireless network is very quick to install, take down, and move to a new location.

Security and Health Concerns

Wireless networks are usually accompanied by security and health
concerns. A network that uses IR signals, while it is limited to line-
of-sight transmissions, has advantages in both these areas.

IR transmissions do not go through walls or floors. Therefore, if anyone is going to illegally tap an IR network that does not include
building-to-building transmissions, they must be physically present
in the office space.

Tapping a network that spans buildings is somewhat less difficult
because all a network cracker needs to do is place a receiver in the
transmission beam to intercept the signal. However, the IR beam
between buildings is only 1–2° wide and an interception device
must be placed directly in the beam to trap the signal. When an IR
beam is disrupted in this way, the network signal is lost. Short disruptions in the signal can be handled by the Ethernet protocols, but
long disruptions—those long enough for a cracker to obtain useful
information—are readily detected because normal network transmissions cease.

People are becoming increasingly concerned about the role of electrical signals in causing cancer, especially where high-voltage signals are involved. It is certainly true that a wireless network adds to the signals that are traveling unseen in the air about us. However, IR network signals are light waves, not electricity, and have no health risks associated with them.

Part Three

Equipping an Ethernet with Hardware and Software

In this part we are going to move above the Ethernet Physical layer and look at the hardware and software that are available to run on that network. In Chapter 7 we will look at the wide variety of network devices that you might decide to attach to an Ethernet. Chapter 8 presents additional material about the major data communications protocols that can be used with an Ethernet and an overview of the network operating systems that provide those protocols.

Chapter 9 looks at setting up peer-to-peer networking in Windows and Macintosh environments, providing a simple way to share files and printers without dedicated servers. In Chapter 10 we will look at network management considerations. Finally, Chapter 11 considers software for monitoring the performance of a network and for discovering what devices are connected to a network.

7

Network Devices

Throughout this book we have been referring to the hardware that is connected to an Ethernet as network devices. In this chapter we will explore the types of hardware you can place on a network and alternatives for that hardware.

Workstations

Virtually any current microcomputer can be used as a network workstation, but today there are a couple of options that you can consider in addition to a standard desktop computer, including laptop computers and what is currently known as a *thin client*.

On-Site Laptop Support

First, you may want to make it possible for laptop computer users to connect directly to the network whenever they are in the office. To do this, you need to provide a work area for the laptop. Then, the laptop will need a PCMCIA adapter, such as that in Figure 7-1, for Ethernet support. The cable attached to the adapter will then plug directly into a wall outlet.

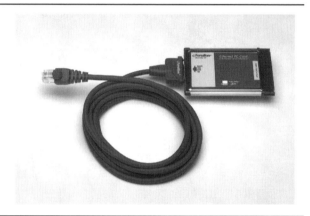

Figure 7-1:   A PCMCIA Ethernet adapter card for a laptop computer (courtesy of Farallon Corp.)

Some users are uncomfortable with the large connector required by a typical PCMCIA adapter. To get away without the external connector, you can purchase an adapter such as the RealPort (from Xircom) in Figure 7-2. Notice that this adapter takes up two Type II PCMCIA slots but in exchange provides both a 10BASE-T connection and a modem. (The third port is a pass-through for the telephone line.)

If a laptop does not have PCMCIA slots, then you can consider using a parallel port adapter, such as the one in Figure 7-3, on an Intel-based laptop. Such adapters usually have a pass-through port so that a printer can be connected to the laptop even when the adapter is in use. Parallel port adapters are becoming harder to find because of the pervasiveness of PCMCIA slots, but you can find them if you look at places such as *http://www.pricewatch.com*.

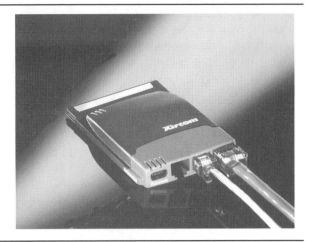

Figure 7-2:   A PCMCIA adapter that does not need an external connector (courtesy of Xircom)

Figure 7-3:   A parallel port adapter for a laptop without PCMCIA slots (courtesy of Xircom)

Note: Parallel port adapters can also be used on desktop devices that have no available slots for an internal NIC.

Thin Clients

In the past few years, there has been a great deal of discussion on using devices that are not complete computers for network devices. These *thin clients* have a CPU and may be able to process data locally, but they have no floppy drive or CD-ROM drive. They may or may not have a hard drive. The thin client machine loads all of its software over the network from a file server and processes data on the local machine. Then, the thin client typically stores its data back on the server.

There are actually three types of thin client machines:

- *Network computer*: A computer with a Java Virtual Machine and a World Wide Web browser. It has its own CPU and can process data retrieved from a server.
- *NetPC*: A stand-alone PC with a hard drive but no floppy or CD-ROM drives. Typically, the system is locked down in such a way that the user cannot make changes to it. A netPC can do local processing but must load software onto its hard drive from a server.
- *Windows-based terminal*: A device with no local processing power. It is designed to access Windows programs stored and executed on a server through the Windows Terminal Server program. It can run non-Windows programs only with the help of an add-on program called MetaFrame (produced by Citrix Systems).

What is the advantage to a thin client? There are several advantages touted by those who support this approach.

- A thin client is slightly cheaper than a stand-alone PC. If all the software a user needs is available over the network or if a user will only be interacting with the Internet and Java applications, there is no need to pay for extra, unnecessary hardware.
- Thin clients are designed specifically for network use and contain firmware to make it possible for a network administrator to access the machine from a central location.

The network administrator can then troubleshoot downed network nodes and make some repairs without needing to travel to the user's location.

♦ A thin client is less complex than a stand-alone PC and therefore less susceptible to hardware problems. It therefore cuts down on the total cost of ownership of the machine.

♦ A thin client is less vulnerable to both hardware and software "tinkering" by end users and therefore less likely to develop problems that require repairs or software reinstallations. This cuts down on calls to an organization's help desk, also bringing down the total cost of ownership.

♦ A thin client provides added security because the user cannot download proprietary information to removable media (and perhaps cannot even store it on a local hard drive).

♦ A thin client can cut down on network traffic, especially if processing is being done on the server. In that case, only keystrokes are sent over the network, rather than large amounts of data.

However, the price difference between a low-end desktop PC and a thin client has not been as dramatic as was originally anticipated, especially now that reasonably powerful stand-alone PCs can be purchased for under $1000. A thin client is also not suited for users who have high-end processing needs, such as those working with high-end graphics, CAD/CAM, or video. Nonetheless, for users who need what is essentially a terminal rather than a stand-alone PC, a thin client can be a cost-effective alternative.

Shared Printers

One of the benefits of a network is the ability to share expensive, high-speed printers with everyone on the network. Such shared printers are typically known as *print servers*: hardware, software, or a combination of both that manage a shared network printer. Printers are considerably slower than the devices that send them information.

Therefore, when a printer is shared by all devices on a network or network segment, there needs to be some way to store the print files as they are sent to the printer and then send them to the printer as the printer becomes available.

A print server must *spool* print jobs as they arrive. Typically, this means storing the print files on a disk. The print server must also monitor the printer and determine when it is ready to accept another job. The print server then sends the job to the printer. Users generally have access to the *print queue* (the list of jobs waiting to be printed) and can see all waiting jobs, cancel their jobs, or delay the printing of their jobs.

There are several different ways to configure a print server, depending on whether the printer is connected directly to the network as an independent network device or whether it is connected to a workstation on the network. The hardware and software you may need also depend on which network protocols you are using.

Ethernet-Compatible Printers

Many workgroup printers (usually laser printers) either are sold today with an Ethernet NIC already installed or are capable of accepting an Ethernet NIC. Such a printer can be connected directly to the network as an independent network device.

However, an Ethernet NIC in a workstation does not provide print spooling. To use a printer equipped with standard Ethernet connectivity, you must provide print spooling in some other way. How this happens depends on the operating system and network protocol you are using.

♦ Windows: With Windows 95 and 98, print spooling is handled by the operating system when a printer is connected directly to the computer. However, a network printer must have its own spooling capabilities if you are using TCP/IP for network communications. Often, this takes the form of spooling software that is stored on a hard disk attached to the printer and runs on the print-er's CPU. (Remember that laser printers are really spe-cial-purpose computers, with CPUs and RAM of their own.) If you are using AppleTalk, then the workstation software spools print jobs on the local machine and de-tects when a job can be sent to the printer.

Note: If you are using Novell NetWare, then even a network-compatible printer must be connected directly to a computer that acts as a print server. See the next section of this chapter for details.

- ♦ UNIX: The UNIX spooler, lp, handles spooling locally and detects when a network printer is available to print a job.
- ♦ Macintosh OS: The Macintosh OS also spools locally and can detect over the network when a printer is available to print a job.

PC-Based Print Servers

If your printer cannot be connected to the network as a stand-alone device, that does not mean that you cannot share that printer. The solution is to connect the printer to a PC, which in turn acts as a print server. Workstations send their print jobs to the PC acting as a print server. Software on that PC spools the jobs and sends them to the printer as it becomes available.

Network operating systems such as Novell NetWare and Windows NT are designed to support PC-based print servers. You can also purchase third-party software for print servers, such as I-Queue! Server for Windows 95 from Infinite Technologies, which allows Windows 95 workstations to act as print servers for either Novell or NT networks.

The advantage of this approach is that you have a central location for managing the print queue. Printer administrators (who may be the same people as network administrators) have access to the print server software running on the PC and can reschedule and delete print jobs as needed.

Because printers are so much slower than computers, a PC acting as a print server does not need to be a particularly fast computer. This is therefore a very good way to use an older PC that would otherwise be discarded. (A 486-based PC or a 68040- or 86030-based Macintosh makes an excellent print server.) The cost of the print server is therefore limited to the cost of the server software, which may come as part of your network operating system.

External Print Servers

If you cannot dedicate a PC to act as a print server, you can attach a non-network-compatible printer to a network through an external print server, a stand-alone device like that in Figure 7-4. Such devices cost anywhere between $150 and $500. If you do not happen to have an extra PC around that you can dedicate as a print server, then this is a much lower cost alternative to purchasing a complete PC.

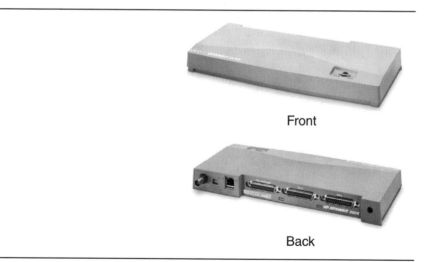

Front

Back

Figure 7-4: **A stand-alone external print server (courtesy of Hewlett-Packard Corp.)**

There are some additional advantages to stand-alone printer servers:

♦ Most of today's external print servers provide web browser–based management software so that the print server can be managed by anyone on the network from his or her desktop workstation.
♦ As a single-purpose device, a print server is less likely to need ongoing maintenance than a PC. Support costs will generally be less than for a PC.
♦ Print servers use less electricity than PCs and therefore cost less to operate.
♦ Print servers generate less heat than PCs and therefore help keep air conditioning costs down.

An external print server has up to three standard parallel and/or serial ports for connecting to the network. Some also come equipped with AUI ports. The print server itself becomes a network device; it will be equipped with a 10BASE-T, 100BASE-T, 10BASE2, and/or LocalTalk port. Most external print servers also ship with software for managing the print queue that can be run on any workstation on the network.

An external print server is usually designed to be compatible with a specific set of network operating systems. Before purchasing one, you should therefore make sure that your particular software is supported.

Internal Print Servers

Some printers that do not come with an Ethernet NIC can instead accept an internal print spooler like the one in Figure 7-5. Expansion boards of this type provide fast print spooling. The print queue can be managed from a network workstation.

The drawback to internal print spoolers is that they are proprietary. In other words, you must purchase a board that is designed specifically for your brand of printer. In particular, you will find a wide

Figure 7-5:   An internal print spooler (courtesy of Hewlett-Packard Corp.)

range of internal print servers available for Hewlett-Packard printers, including some that provide a parallel port for attaching a second printer. However, if you do not happen to have a printer for which an internal print server is available, then you must use either an external print server or a PC as a print server.

File Servers

The term *file server* can be applied to any number of devices, each of which provides a repository for shared files. You may also hear such devices called an *application server* (a file server that contains applications for network users to run), a *database server* (a file server that runs a database management system and provides data management capabilities to a user), or a *web server* (a file server that is hosting a web site).

There are several basic architectures for file servers.

♦ A stand-alone computer dedicated to acting as a file server: This computer has a monitor and keyboard and can be managed by someone working directly with the server. Although most new Ethernets use high-end PCs as file servers, older organizations with legacy mainframes and minicomputers have turned those machines into file servers, rather than spending money on new hardware.

♦ A "headless" PC with no monitor or keyboard: This type of file server, such as the Snap! Server in Figure 7-6, must be managed from another PC on the network. The advantage of a server of this type is that it comes completely "plug and play" ready. You simply plug in a power cord (#1 in Figure 7-6), insert either a 10BASE-T or a 100BASE-T cable into the back (#2 in Figure 7-6), and turn on the power switch (#3 in Figure 7-6); it is ready to mount on the user's desktop immediately. The Snap! Server is compatible with Windows 95, Windows NT, Novell NetWare, and UNIX Network File System (NFS) right out of the box. It can be used with Macintosh networks with the addition of networking software known as DAVE.

Note: Like many network devices today, the Snap! Server uses web browser–based management software. This means that it is not limited to a single computing platform.

Note: You can read more about DAVE in Chapter 10 in the section covering Macintosh access to Windows NT servers.

♦ A virtual server: Using software such as MangoSoft Corp.'s Medley98, you can allocate a portion of the hard disk of each of up to 25 PCs to be part of a *virtual server*. For example, if you have ten PCs on your network and you allocate 1 Gb on each hard disk to the virtual server, the entire network will have access to a 10 Gb server, which appears as a local drive to each user. Medley98 keeps two copies of each file placed on the virtual server,

Front

Back

Figure 7-6:   A Snap! Server file server (courtesy of Merdian Data, Inc.)

providing backup access to files if one of the machines happens to be down. Medley98 has two limitations: It can handle a maximum of only 25 machines and, at the time this book was written it was only compatible with Windows 95 and Windows 98. (MangoSoft had announced a forthcoming Windows NT version but was not planning to support UNIX or the Macintosh OS.)

♦ A nondedicated file server: In a type of networking known as *peer-to-peer*, any workstation with a hard disk on the network can temporarily become a file server. A user mounts the hard disk of another workstation on his or her desktop and gains access to the files on that hard disk. You will read more about peer-to-peer networking in Chapter 8.

Dedicated file servers are the most common type of file servers. Peer-to-peer networking is generally appropriate only for occasional file sharing because it slows down the workstation whose hard disk is being used by others on the network.

Most networks use their fastest machines as file servers. File servers are also connected to the network using the fastest Ethernet connections available. For example, Gigabit Ethernet is currently designed primarily for server use. The idea is that you use fiber optic cabling to connect a group of file servers (often called a *server farm*) to a switch or router, which then uses Fast Ethernet or standard Ethernet to communicate with the other devices on the network. A sample configuration of this type is diagrammed in Figure 7-7.

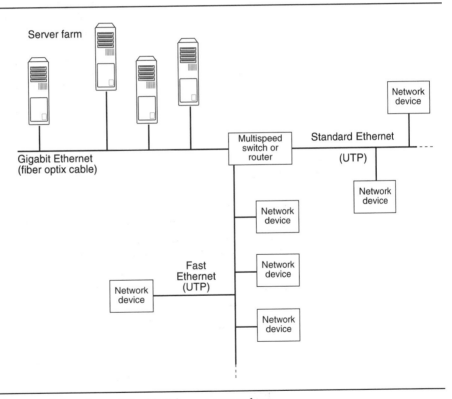

Figure 7-7: **A network based on a Gigabit Ethernet server farm**

Should a file server do more than one thing? For example, does it make sense to use the same computer to provide a place from which users can load applications and on which to run your database engine? This is a tough question to answer. It depends on your individual software needs and how much money you have to spend.

Database processing is a disk-intensive activity, as is serving up applications. If database performance is important to you, then you will probably want to dedicate a server to the database management system (DBMS). On the down side, network traffic between the database server and the application server can mitigate performance gains.

In most cases, web servers should also be placed on dedicated machines, since serving up web data is both disk and processor intensive. In addition, if your network is hosting a busy web site, you may find that you need several copies of the web server (*mirrors*) and that your web server software will need to route users to the mirrors to balance the network load.

If you can afford it, dedicated servers connected by Gigabit Ethernet generally will provide optimal performance for heavily trafficked networks. However, if that type of arrangement is beyond your budget or if your network is small or not heavily used for real-time processing, then you may decide to house your database server on the same machine as your application server. At the very least, this will minimize network traffic. You can then dedicate your fastest machine to serving programs and the database.

Fax and E-mail Servers

Fax and e-mail servers are computers dedicated to handling fax and e-mail communications. Neither of these machines performs time-sensitive operations. (Fax machines rarely transmit faster than 9600 bps, and e-mail is essentially a batch operation.) Therefore, this is another instance where older computers can serve a useful purpose.

Fax Servers

A fax server is simply a computer connected to a modem that dials out to send faxes and answers incoming fax calls. The simplest architecture is to add an old modem to an old computer, connect the modem to the phone line, and connect the computer to the network. For example, the author's fax server is a Macintosh SE/30 purchased for $175 and a 14.4 modem left over from an upgrade. The only other cost in setting up the fax server was the network card for the computer (about $100).

> *Note: The reliability of older computers is absolutely amazing. Assuming that you turn them on and leave them on 24 hours a day, 7 days a week, they will run for years. (This assumes that you either leave the monitor off or at least turned all the way down so no image is visible.) All you really need to protect them is a good surge suppressor.*

Once the hardware is set up, you can use one of two types of software:

♦ *Traditional fax software*: Runs only on the fax server. All faxes come into the fax server; users must pick them up off that computer. To send a fax, a user must create a fax file and then transfer it over the network to the fax server's "out box" folder. Given that most modems ship with single-user fax software, this is a very inexpensive solution, albeit a bit clumsy.

♦ *Network fax software*: Installed on both client machines and the fax server. To send a fax, the user creates the fax on his or her workstation and the fax is automatically sent to the fax server for transmission. Depending on the software, incoming faxes may or may not be automatically routed to recipients. This is an easier solution to use, but considerably more expensive, especially since it is usually priced per user.

E-mail Servers

As mentioned earlier, e-mail is basically a batch operation. Messages come in and are stored on the computer that receives them. Users pick up waiting messages over the network at a time convenient for them. Outgoing messages may be sent immediately or may be spooled to the e-mail server's disk and transmitted as a group at pre-set intervals. For example, the default for a UNIX System V system is to send outgoing e-mail twice every hour.

An e-mail server therefore does not need to be a fast computer, but it needs significant hard drive storage to handle both incoming and outgoing messages. It also requires e-mail software installed on the server and on all workstations from which e-mail will be sent or received.

> *Note: It is beyond the scope of this book to discuss specific e-mail server software products. There are a myriad of choices, many of which provide cross-platform client software for mixed networks. In addition, most NOSs include e-mail software. You can therefore use the e-mail capabilities of your NOS, use a free-ware implementation, or purchase a commercial e-mail product. Pricing for commercial products is typically per user.*

CD-ROM Servers

With the arrival of large databases on CD-ROM, many organizations have been looking for equipment that can mount many CDs simultaneously and share those disks among multiple users. *CD-ROM servers* are special-purpose hardware designed for that function.

Originally, the only way to make multiple CD-ROMs available on a network was to use a jukebox arrangement whereby a CD was selected from a collection of CDs to be mounted in a single drive. This is still a viable solution for CDs that are not accessed frequently.

Currently, however, it is more common to use a CD-ROM tower that contains multiple CD-ROM drives for discs that are accessed regularly. For example, the Maxtet/CD Enterprise tower in Figure 7-8 can be configured with up to 64 CD-ROM drives. Dedicated CD-ROM servers do, however, cost more than CD-ROM jukeboxes.

Figure 7-8: **A CD-ROM tower that provides multiple-user access to multiple CDs (courtesy of Optical Access International)**

Depending on the type of CD-ROM server you purchase, it may be usable as a stand-alone network device or it may need to be connected to a server. When the CD-ROM tower is a stand-alone device, it will have its own CPU, main memory, and hard drive. To facilitate access by multiple users to the same CD-ROM, the CD-ROM server caches frequently accessed information such as disc directories on its hard disk.

Because a CD-ROM server is basically a headless computer, it is accompanied by management software that runs on a workstation on the network. Users see the CD-ROMs as individual disk volumes. However, management software allows a network administrator to impose access restrictions on specific CDs in the tower.

CD-ROM drives are noticeably slower than hard drives and Ethernet networks. They also often contain large graphics, video, or audio files. You would therefore expect that performance of a CD-ROM tower would be rather slow. This is indeed true. However, in most cases, the limiting factor is the CD-ROM drives rather than the network. You may therefore decide that the convenience of having large numbers of CDs available to networked users outweighs performance considerations.

CD-ROM servers are generally compatible with a wide range of network operating systems, making them plug-and-play devices similar to the Snap! Server described earlier in this chapter. For example, the Maxtet/CD Enterprise supports Novell NetWare, Microsoft Windows NT/LAN Manager, OS/2 LAN Server, AppleShare, and World Wide Web browsers.

8

Network Protocols and Operating Systems

The software that you choose for an Ethernet is as important as the hardware that carries your data communications messages. In this chapter we will look at the protocols that make up the major protocol stacks. For the most part, the benefit of reading this is to become familiar with the protocol acronyms and where they fit into the stacks. You may never need to know the details of how those protocols do their jobs, but the functionality of a great deal of networking software is expressed in terms of the protocols it supports. You may therefore find it difficult to purchase appropriate software if you do not at least know the basic function of the major protocols.

Most networking protocols are supplied as part of network operating systems. The second portion of this chapter therefore provides an overview of the major network operating systems and the services they provide for an Ethernet.

Major Network Protocols

Network protocols are often somewhat cynically characterized as "alphabet soup." Each protocol has a name and an acronym, and it is almost certain that by the time you finish reading this section, your head will be reeling with three- and four-letter combinations. Nonetheless, it is important for you to become at least somewhat familiar with the major protocols and the services they provide to a network.

> Note: Keep in mind that the protocols described in this section are all implemented in software and, with the exception of NIC drivers, are independent of the physical media over which they run. Although we will be talking about them in the context of an Ethernet, they can also be used, for example, over Token Ring cabling.

To understand the function of some of the major protocols, you will need to understand the difference between *connection-oriented, acknowledged connectionless,* and *unacknowledged connectionless* exchanges. A connection-oriented exchange assumes that there is a *virtual circuit*—a single identified transmission path—between a sender and a receiver and that every packet that is part of a single message travels by that path. The packet transfer includes error checking and flow-control services.

Connectionless exchanges do not have to use a single path for every packet. Instead, each packet is routed by the most efficient pathway. Unacknowledged connectionless service provides no error checking or flow-control services. It also does not let the sender know that a packet has arrived. However, there is usually some protocol higher in the stack that does so. Acknowledged connectionless service lets the sender know that a packet has been received, but still does no error checking or flow control.

As you will see, protocols in the lower layers of a protocol stack provide connectionless services. Upper layers provide connection-oriented services so that a message exchange appears to an application as if it were traveling in the same route throughout its passage through the network. A message will travel by only one type of service.

Connectionless service means that a routing decision needs to be made by a switch or router independently for each packet. Connection-oriented service determines the route for a message when the first packet arrives at the switch or router. The switch or router stores the route and then looks it up as each subsequent packet arrives. Unless there is a major change in network load during the transmission of a single message, connection-oriented service is generally more efficient than connectionless service. Because it includes error checking, it also provides a more reliable level of service.

TCP/IP

There was a time when data communications experts felt that the OSI protocol stack would become the model for all data communications protocols. However, that was before the Internet became as ubiquitous as it is now. Today the TCP/IP protocol stack that you first saw in Chapter 1 is the most widely used set of protocols.

There are many protocols in the TCP/IP protocol stack. Some of the most commonly used can be found in Table 8-1. As you can see, most of the protocols can be found at the application level in support of a wide variety of network activities.

The TCP/IP protocol stack is available with virtually every NOS. You can therefore choose to use either the NOS's native protocols or TCP/IP. At the time this book was written, the trend was toward using TCP/IP.

TCP/IP layer	Name	Acronym	Function/Purpose
Network	Internet Protocol	IP	Provides connectionless service along with logical network addressing, packet switching, and dynamic routing.
Transport	Transmission Control Protocol	TCP	Provides connection-oriented service, including error correction and flow control.
	User Datagram Protocol	UDP	Provides connectionless service. Is considered unreliable and therefore not heavily used at this time.
Application	Network File System	NFS	Supports file sharing between networks.
	Simple Mail Transfer Protocol	SMTP	Supports the transfer of e-mail.
	File Transfer Protocol	FTP	Supports file transfer.
	Hypertext Transfer Protocol	HTTP	Supports the transfer of hypertext documents (i.e., documents containing HTML).
	Simple Network Management Protocol	SNMP	Supports basic functions for managing network devices. Many commercial network management products are based on SNMP.
	Telnet		Supports remote terminal sessions.
	Multipurpose Internet Mail Extensions	MIME	Supports the attachment of multiple files to e-mail messages.
	Hypertext Markup Language	HTML	Supports the creation of hypertext documents for network transfer and display.

Table 8-1:   TCP/IP protocols

IPX/SPX

IPX and SPX are platform-independent protocols. They form the basis of the IPX/SPX protocol stack, the native protocol stack of Novell NetWare. This stack maps rather nicely to the seven-layer OSI Reference Model. The layers and their major protocols are summarized for you in Table 8-2.

> *Note: The Novell NetWare protocol stack was originally based on a four-layer stack developed jointly with Apple Computer in 1989. From the bottom up, the original layers were as follows: a physical layer that included NIC driver software, a data link layer, a layer containing server protocols, and a layer containing NetWare services. IPX and SPX themselves, however, were based on work done at Xerox PARC.*

IPX and SPX provide connectionless and connection-mode packet transfers, respectively. IPX in particular is available outside of the Novell NetWare environment and can be used with other network operating systems to support file transfer over a network. For example, the Macintosh implementation of IPX—a system extension known as MacIPX—can be used to exchange files with a Windows 95 or Windows 98 machine (which also comes with its own IPX implementation).

VINES

VINES is a proprietary protocol stack developed by Banyan for its VINES network operating system—discussed later in this chapter—that maps to the OSI seven-layer model (see Table 8-3). The major departure from the OSI model comes at the Data Link layer, where VINES's Fragmentation Protocol (FRP) is housed. In the OSI mode, packet disassembly and reassembly is handled at the Session layer.

The heart of the VINES protocol stack is VINES Internet Protocol (VIP). It is similar in function to IP in that it supports the actual transfer of the fragmented packets across the network. Connectionless and connection-oriented services are provided by the Inter Process Communication Protocol (IPC) and the Sequenced Packet Protocol (SPP), respectively.

OSI layer	Name	Acronym	Function/Purpose
Physical	Multiple link interface driver	MLID	A NIC driver that can support any kind of network packet
Data Link	Link support layer	LSL	Identifies the type of packet received and routes it to the appropriate protocol in the Network layer above.
Network	Internet packet exchange	IPX	Performs translations between physical addressing from layers below to logical addressing for layers above. Also performs connectionless routing functions.
Transport	Sequenced packet exchange	SPX	Provides a connection-oriented service between the addresses identified by IPX.
Session,	NetWare Core Protocol	NCP	Server management
Presentation, and	Service Advertising Protocol	SAP	Broadcasts NetWare services available to network devices.
Application	NETBios emulation		Support for IBM connectivity
	STREAMS		Connection to services in the upper network layers
	Remote procedure call	RPC	Provides transparent access to remote resources.
	Message handling service	MHS[a]	Provides a message delivery system.
	BTRIEVE[b]		Provides database support.
	NetWare loadable modules	NLMs[c]	Application software and utilities that can be loaded to extend NetWare's functionality

Table 8-2:   The IPX/SPX protocol stack as implemented by Novell NetWare

[a]   MHS is not strictly a communications protocol, but a platform-independent message-handling service

[b]   BTRIEVE is not strictly a communications protocol, but multiplatform database software.

[c]   NLMs are also not strictly communications protocols, but programs that can run on NetWare servers

OSI layer	Name	Acronym	Function/Purpose
Physical	Medica Access Protocols (network dependent)		
Data Link	Fragmentation Protocol	FRP	Breaks packets into smaller pieces for transport over the network and reassembles them when they are received.
Network	VINES Internet Protocol	VIP	Provides delivery of packets.
	Routing Update Protocol	RTP	Distributes network topology information among servers.
	Address Resolution Protocol	ARP	Assigns addresses to clients as they enter the network.
	Internet Control Protocol	ICP	Provides information on unreachable nodes; provides data on routing "costs."
Transport	Inter Process Communication Protocol	IPC	Provides connectionless datagram transfer services.
	Sequenced Packet Protocol	SPP	Provides connection-oriented message transfer services.
Session Presentation	Remote Procedure Call	RPC	Provides transparent access to remote resources.
Application	File services		
	Print services		
	StreetTalk		Binds names assigned to network devices to physical device addresses.

Table 8-3:   VINES protocols

AppleTalk

Like the Novell NetWare protocol stack, AppleTalk is designed around the OSI Reference Model (see Table 8-4). It provides Physical layer drivers for three MAC systems (LocalTalk, Ethernet, and Token Ring) as well as a complete set of packet transfer and server management protocols.

AppleTalk is most useful with an all-Macintosh network or with a network that includes primarily Macintoshes and a few PCs. It runs on top of Ethernet hardware as easily as it does on LocalTalk hardware. To switch from the slower LocalTalk cabling, all you have to do is replace the wiring and switch to an EtherTalk driver. The remainder of the protocols are hardware independent.

NetBEUI

NetBEUI (NetBIOS extended user interface) is an alternative to TCP/IP developed by IBM in 1985 and supplied with Windows for Workgroups, Windows 95, Windows 98, and Windows NT. It was originally intended for network segments containing between 20 and 200 devices. Network segments would then be connected with gateways.

NetBEUI has been optimized for small LAN segments. It is therefore very fast for file transfers within a given segment. It also has good error control and requires very little main memory. However, it cannot be routed and transmission speeds for large networks, especially those connected into a WAN, are poor.

Windows comes with NetBEUI installed. It can also coexist with TCP/IP on the same computer. Some installations use NetBEUI for file transfers within the same network segment but switch to TCP/IP for file transfers that require routing or the use of a WAN.

If both protocols are available on the same Windows machine, you can configure the operating system to indicate which protocol should be used first. When NetBEUI is the first protocol to be used,

OSI layer	Name	Acronym	Function/Purpose
Physical and	LocalTalk		Software driver for running over LocalTalk cabling.
Data Link	EtherTalk		Software driver for running over Ethernet cabling.
	TokenTalk		Software driver for running over Token Ring cabling.
Network	Datagram Delivery Protocol	DDP	Connectionless routing between source and destination.
	Routing Table Maintenance Protocol	RTMP	Takes care of building routing tables (also operates at the Transport layer).
Transport	AppleTalk Transaction Protocol	ATP	Provides connectionless transfer of packets between protocol stacks.
Session	AppleTalk Data Stream Protocol	ADSP	Provides connection-oriented packet transfer (also operates at the Transport layer).
	AppleTalk Session Protocol	ASP	Works with ATP to provide reliable packet transfers; provides the error checking and flow control for ATP's connectionless service.
	AppleTalk Printer Access Protocol	PAP	Provides support for networked printers.
Presentation	AppleTalk Filing Protocol	AFP	Supports network file sharing.
Application	AppleShare		The Apple network operating system that provides file sharing (using AFP), security, and so on.

Table 8-4:   AppleTalk protocols

a Windows NT server will automatically use NetBEUI within the same segment and TCP/IP for moving packets between segments through a switch or router.

> *Note: Some network administrators consider NetBEUI to be a "nasty" protocol because it is hard to work with. Although it has been a part of Windows for some time, it is no longer as widely used as TCP/IP.*

Network Operating Systems

As you have read, a network operating system, or NOS, is software that manages the sharing of files over a network. A network operating system) is therefore usually responsible for the following:

- Maintaining user accounts and passwords to provide some level of security for the network
- File management on the server
- Scheduling of programs and services to be run at regular intervals
- Printing
- File locking and synchronization
- Accounting

A network operating system may be an add-on to a single-user operating system or it may be integrated into a complete operating system product.

Novell NetWare

Novell NetWare was the first widely used network operating system. Early releases made it possible to network computers running MS-DOS, a single-user operating system that had absolutely no native networking capabilities.

Versions 3.x and 4.x, which are still widely used, rely on the proprietary Novell NetWare protocol stack. However, NetWare 5—the version released about the time this book was written—has taken a different approach. Novell recognized the overwhelming acceptance of TCP/IP and has therefore switched its primary protocol support to the Internet protocols. However, NetWare 5 still provides support for the Novell protocol stack to ensure backward compatibility with existing installations.

As with any NOS, NetWare requires two types of software: server software installed on all servers on the network, and client software installed on all workstations.

Network Management and Server Software

Like all NOSs, NetWare provides software to manage servers and to manage the overall network. The network as a whole appears to a network administrator as a single directory tree. This is the visual component of NetWare Directory Services (NDS), which makes it possible for network administrators to keep track of all resources on the network. The window in the center of Figure 8-1, for example, shows the directories available on a server named NW5_SYS.

In addition to directory services, NetWare's administrative capabilities include creating and maintaining user accounts (including user security), creating and maintaining print servers, and collecting and preparing network-user accounting information. In Figure 8-2, for example, you can see the way in which NetWare 5.0 handles establishing domain name services for groups of users.

NetWare is available from Novell Corp. for Intel-based servers. A Linux version has been ported by Caldera Corp. In addition, the MARS project is working on a version of all of the free UNIX implementations.

Client Software

Client software is available for MS-DOS, Windows 3.x, OS/2, Macintosh, Unix, Windows NT, Windows 95, and Windows 98. All of the preceding are supported by both the Novell product and the

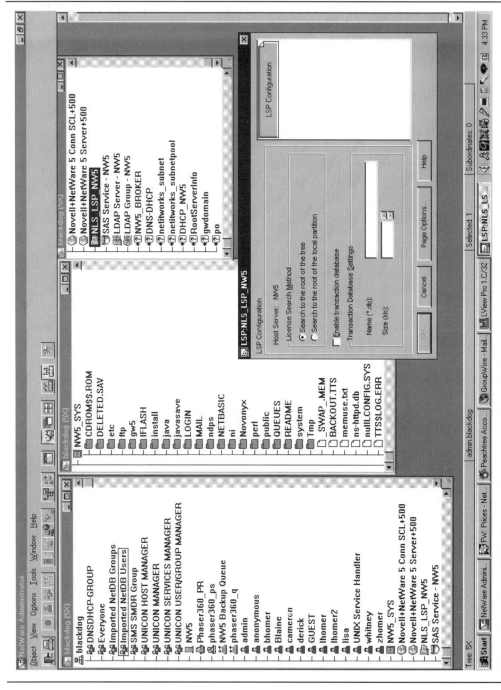

Figure 8-1:   Novell NetWare 5.0 directory services display

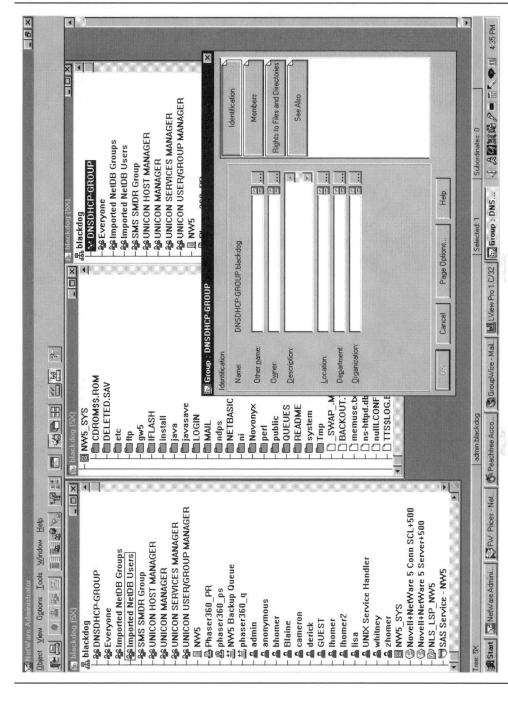

Figure 8-2: Novell NetWare 5.0 users and groups display

Caldera product. NetWare is therefore a good choice for a multi-platform environment.

> *Note: The NetWare client software is shipped as a part of the Windows family of operating systems. Nonetheless, you must purchase the server software if you are going to use Novell Net-Ware as your network operating system. In addition, many network experts believe that the Windows client implementation is weak; Novell recommends that you use its client software instead.*

NetWare clients can be configured to use any of the following combinations of protocols:

- ♦ IP only: Clients configured for IP only operate in a TCP/IP environment. However, if IPX compatibility mode software is installed, such clients can access servers using the NetWare protocols.
- ♦ IP + IPX: Clients configured in this way can access servers using either TCP/IP or the NetWare protocols.
- ♦ IPX only: Clients configured solely for IPX can only access servers that are using the NetWare protocols.

Which you use for your clients depends, of course, on the types of existing servers you have.

Banyan VINES

One of the earliest network operating systems was VINES (VIrtual NEtwork System), produced and sold by Banyan. Today, VINES is a multiprotocol, multiplatform NOS. Early versions of VINES used only the proprietary VINES protocol stack, which you read about earlier in this chapter. Currently, however, VINES supports TCP/IP along with its original protocol stack.

VINES directory services are managed through a Windows application called StreetTalk. As you can see in Figure 8-3, the program provides a tree-structured display of network resources. Other basic

VINES services include network management, support for server-to-server communication, printer support, and security. VINES can also work in a serverless environment, where workstations are simply connected by switches or routers.

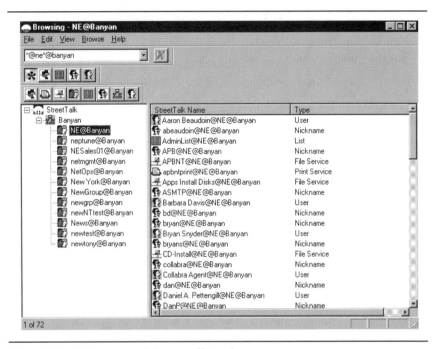

Figure 8-3:   Using VINES StreetTalk to view system resources

VINES provides client software for MS-DOS, Windows 3.1, Windows 95, Windows NT, and Macintosh OS. It is therefore a viable NOS choice for multiplatform networks.

Windows NT

Windows NT (or Windows 2000, depending on which version you are using) is actually two operating systems: Windows NT Server and Windows NT Workstation. The Server component provides the typical NOS functions. Networked computers can run NT Workstation or any other operating system that has client software able to access an NT file server.

Note: At the time this book was written, Windows 2000 was still under development, but may be available as you read this. The comments and illustrations in this section relate to that version.

Note: Windows 95 and Windows 98 include peer-to-peer networking, which is discussed in the next section of this chapter, as well as client software that can access an NT server. However, they cannot act as dedicated servers. For that you need Windows NT.

Windows NT Server provides management services for servers, desktop computers, and network resources. One of the primary resource management interfaces is the Active Directory Manager, which provides a hierarchical view of all user resources on the network. In Figure 8-4, for example, a group of users named Research is highlighted on the left side of the window. On the right, the network manager can see all users who are part of that group.

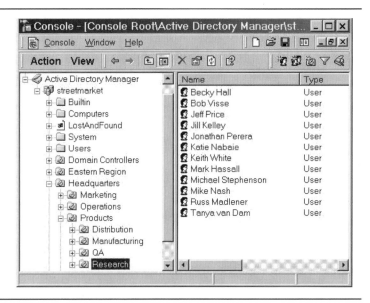

Figure 8-4:   Windows 2000 Active Directory Manager

Additional workstation and user management is provided by the Group Policy Editor (Figure 8-5). With this software a network administrator can deploy application software and automate management tasks such as operating system updates, application installation, installing user profiles, and locking down desktop systems to prevent users from changing them.

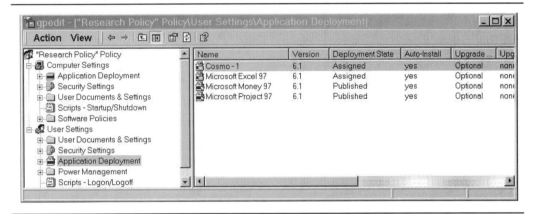

Figure 8-5: Windows 2000 Group Policy Editor

Hardware management is provided by the Computer Manager (Figure 8-6). The interface is very similar to that used by all Windows operating systems to configure system hardware. The overall intent is for Windows NT to provide network managers with a familiar GUI to make it easier for them to keep track of the organization of the network.

Like most network computing environments today, Windows NT has moved toward providing significant support for Internet-based technologies. For example, as well as supporting typical networked, shared printers, NT also supports Internet Printing Protocol (IPP), which allows users to print directly to a URL. Other web-related NT services include the following:

- ◆ Active Server Pages (ASP): Support for the development of web-based applications
- ◆ CPU throttling: CPU load balancing when multiple web sites are being hosted on the same server

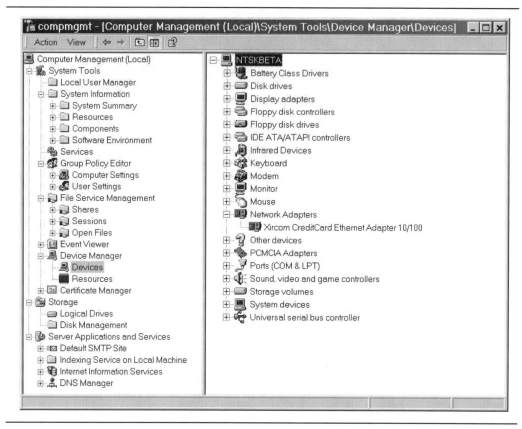

Figure 8-6:   Windows NT 2000 Computer Manager

- ◆ Microsoft Internet Information Server (IIS): Web site hosting
- ◆ Secure Socket Layer (SSL) support: Support for secure web sites

In addition, Windows NT provides extensive support for streaming audio and video.

Note: Macintosh OS computers can be used as clients on a Windows NT network. For more information, see Chapter 10.

UNIX

From its earliest days, UNIX has included networking capabilities. As you saw in Table 8-1, the TCP/IP protocols provide the basis for e-mail, file sharing, and file transfer. A UNIX server requires no special software to support ftp for file transfer or e-mail, for example.

There are many versions of UNIX available. However, a freeware, open-source implementation—Linux—is gaining considerable support in corporations, especially since major database vendors (for example, Oracle and IBM) have ported their products to that particular UNIX flavor. The remainder of the comments in this section therefore apply to using Linux as a server operating system. If you are working with another version of UNIX, then you may find some differences in your particular software.

Linux can function as both a file server and a print server. Like all versions of UNIX, its native networking protocol stack is TCP/IP. However, Linux also supports Service Message Block (SMB), also known as "Samba," to communicate with Windows computers. SMB serves as a replacement for NFS, the traditional UNIX file sharing protocol. Samba is easier to configure than NFS and is generally considered to be more secure.

> *Note: To enable Macintosh OS computers to access a Linux file or print server, you must install an AppleTalk protocol stack on the Linux machine. (There are Macintosh versions of Linux that can, of course, access a Linux server without any special software.) One such stack is Columbia AppleTalk Package, or CAP (free from the University of Melbourne's web site). The other alternative is netatalk, also available at no cost (from the University of Michigan). See Appendix B for URLs.*

The major drawback to using Linux as a file and print server is that setup of users, file sharing privileges, and print sharing is more difficult than with NOSs that operate through a graphic user interface. To configure Linux, you must work at the command line and use a text editor to modify configuration files.

Note: Linux does have a GUI — X Windows — but many con-figuration processes nonetheless must be performed from the command line.

As an example, consider that the setup process involves the following steps:

1. Configure any Windows clients, assigning TCP/IP addresses so that each address on the network is unique. Also be sure to give the computer a unique network name. (Details of how to do this are covered in Chapter 9.)

2. Configure any Linux clients, using procedures similar to those used on the server.

3. Edit the server's */etc/hosts* file to add the names of the hosts on the network.

4. Use the *useradd* program to add each user to the */etc/passwd* and */etc/group* files. The user names must match the names given to the clients.

5. Edit */etc/passwd* to enable logins for each user. (This involves removing the * from the end of the login name.)

6. Log on to the server as each new user and set the password using the */usr/bin/passwd* utility. If users are to be able to log on successfully, the password in the */etc/passwd* file must match the password stored in the client's network configuration.

7. Edit */etc/smb.conf* to add Samba shares for each host configured in step 3. Typically, you create a default share named *pchome* that forces Linux to attempt to match the name of a computer trying to connect with the name of a computer in the */etc/hosts* file. When a match is found, Linux then looks for a match on the user name and password.

The procedure for configuring a print server is similar, in that you must manually alter configuration files and send commands to specific Linux programs.

Although configuration of a Linux server may be more difficult than working with GUI-based NOSs, there are several benefits to making the effort to do the setup.

◆ Linux is freeware. You may pay a small fee (less than $50) for a Linux distribution on CD-ROM, but the source code is available so you can customize your OS.

◆ Linux is cross-platform. There are distributions available for Intel and Motorola microprocessors.

◆ Linux is extremely stable. Once you have the server up and running, maintenance will be minimal.

Note: There are a number of fine books available that discuss setting up a Linux network, most of which include a CD-ROM with a Linux distribution. To find the most current, go to one of the online bookstores and search under "Linux and network-ing."

AppleShare

AppleShare is an add-on to the Macintosh Operating System that manages a dedicated file server. (Peer-to-peer networking, which is native to the Macintosh OS, is discussed in Chapter 9.) Originally, the Macintosh OS used a proprietary file transfer protocol—Apple Filing Protocol (AFP)—but today it also supports TCP/IP.

If you look back at Table 8-4, you will notice that AppleShare is actually just a single protocol at the Application layer in the Apple-Talk protocol stack. The rest of the protocol stack is part of the system software used by every Macintosh (in particular, used to support peer-to-peer networking). Therefore, setting up an Apple-Share file server requires the addition of only that very top layer.

AppleShare IP 6, the most current version of the software when this book was written, provides support for web servers, file servers, e-mail servers, and print servers through a centralized management interface (Figure 8-7). Client software is available for both Macintosh OS and Windows 95 and 98 computers.

Figure 8-7:   The AppleShare management interface

Like other NOSs, AppleShare allows network administrators to establish users and groups of users, assigning access rights and passwords to them as appropriate (see Figure 8-8). In addition, AppleShare allows a network administrator to monitor server activity, as illustrated in Figure 8-9.

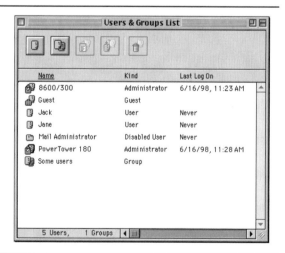

Figure 8-8:   Managing AppleShare users and groups of users

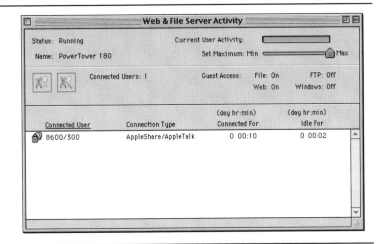

Figure 8-9: Monitoring server activity using an AppleShare network

For Macintosh OS clients, gaining access to an AppleShare file server is no different from peer-to-peer networking. The shared disk volume mounts on the user's desktop like a local volume and can be used as if it were local (within the constraints of the user's access rights to the shared volume).

Windows client software must include the entire AppleTalk protocol stack, which is not included with the Windows 95 and 98 operating systems. It must therefore be loaded into main memory before a Windows user can access an AppleShare file server (much like the way in which TCP/IP and Winsock are loaded at system start-up).

9

Peer-to-Peer Networking

Although most of what you have read to this point assumes that a network contains one or more dedicated servers, for small networks or ad hoc file sharing, dedicated servers may be unnecessary. Windows 95, Windows 98, Windows NT, and Macintosh OS support a type of file sharing known as *peer-to-peer*, where any computer's hard disk can temporarily become a server and be mounted on the desktop of another machine.

> *Note: Peer-to-peer networking is also provided by third-party products such as LANtastic.*

Peer-to-peer networking is less secure than using a dedicated file server. The responsibility for establishing user accounts and passwords is left up to each computer owner, rather than to a network administrator. This type of networking is therefore best suited to small networks where security is not a major concern. It may be

155

unsuitable for even a small installation if the network is connected directly to the Internet, however.

In this chapter you will read about how to set up peer-to-peer networking in each of those operating system environments. Then, you will be introduced to remote control software that allows a networked computer to control another computer on the network. Such software also supports file transfer without mounting a hard drive from another computer.

Windows 95 and 98

Peer-to-peer networking is built into the Windows operating systems. A user who has been given access to all or part of a disk on another Windows machine on the network can access the shared drive as if it were a local drive. Removable media, such as CD-ROMs, can also be shared. In addition, Windows peer-to-peer networking allows the sharing of printers connected directly to a computer.

Setting Up File Sharing

To configure Windows for disk sharing, the user of the computer whose disks will be shared (the computer owner), needs to do at most five things:

- Configure the operating system for networking. (Do this only once unless your hardware changes.)
- Establish a network identity, including an IP address and a computer name. (Do this only once unless it changes.)
- Enable file sharing.
- Choose items to be shared. (Do this each time you want to share disks.)
- Assign access rights to the shared items. (Do this each time you want to share disks.)

Configuring the Computer for Networking

Assuming that a NIC is already installed in a Windows PC, a computer owner must tell Windows which card is present so that the operating system can use the correct driver. If necessary, the owner must also select network client software, choose a protocol stack, and establish a "service" to provide peer-to-peer networking support. All of these steps are handled through the Network control panel (Figure 9-1).

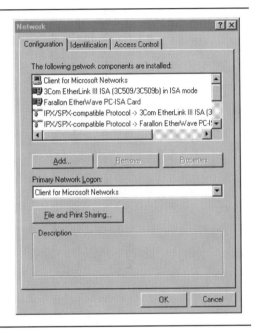

Figure 9-1:   The Windows 95 Network control panel

If you are a computer owner who wants to share files, you first click the Add button to view a list of the types of components that can be added to the system (see Figure 9-2). Then you configure each type of component individually.

Client Software

To install a network client for peer-to-peer networking:

1. Highlight Client in the Select Network Component Type window.

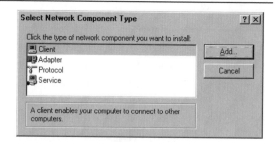

Figure 9-2:   Types of components that can be added to Windows networking

2. Click the Add button. The Select Network Client window appears (see Figure 9-3).

3. Highlight Microsoft in the Manufacturers list.

4. Highlight Client for Microsoft Network in the Network Clients list.

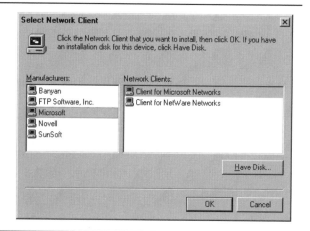

Figure 9-3:   Adding network client software

5. If the client software is on a floppy disk or CD-ROM, click the Have Disk button and select the disk (see Figure 9-4).

6. Click the OK button to install the client software.

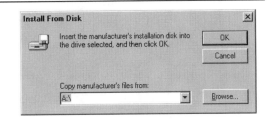

Figure 9-4:   Choosing a disk from which software will be loaded

Network Adapter

To install the correct software driver for the NIC being used in a Windows PC:

1. Highlight Adapter in the Select Network Component Type window.

2. Click the Add button. The Select Network Adapter window appears (see Figure 9-5).

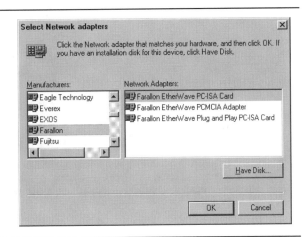

Figure 9-5:   Installing a NIC driver

3. Choose the manufacturer of the adapter in the Manufacturers list.

4. Choose the NIC model in the Network Adapters list.

5. If the NIC driver is on a floppy disk or CD-ROM, click the Have
    Disk button and select the disk.

6. Click the OK button to install the NIC driver.

Network Protocol

To choose the network protocol stack to be used with peer-to-peer
networking:

1. Highlight Protocol in the Select Network Component Type
    window.

2. Click the Add button. The Select Network Protocol window ap-
    pears.

3. Choose Microsoft in the Manufacturers list.

4. Choose TCP/IP in the Network Protocols list (see Figure 9-6).

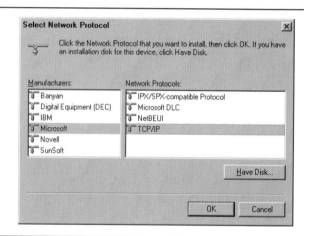

Figure 9-6:   Choosing the TCP/IP protocol stack

5. If the network protocol stack is on a floppy disk or CD-ROM,
    click the Have Disk button and select the disk.

6. Click the OK button to install TCP/IP.

Service

To create a network service for peer-to-peer networking:

1. Highlight Service in the Select Network Component Type window.

2. Click the Add button. The Select Network Service window appears.

3. Click Microsoft in the Manufacturers list.

4. Click File and printer sharing for Microsoft Networks in the Network Services disk (Figure 9-7).

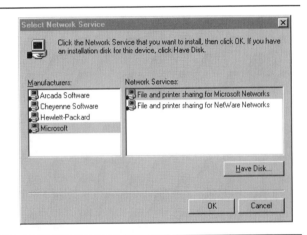

Figure 9-7:   Creating a network service

5. If the service software is on a floppy disk or CD-ROM, click the Have Disk button and select the disk.

6. Click the OK button to create the network service.

> *Note: The Identification and Access Control tabs will not appear in the Network control panel until you have established a service, so be sure to complete this step before attempting to proceed any further.*

Verify Primary User Logon

At this point, you can close the Select Network Component Type window. Make sure that Windows Logon is selected in the Primary Network Logon box in the middle of the Network control panel. If it is not, choose Windows Logon from the drop-down menu.

Setting Network Identity

A Windows computer's network identify has two components: a name and an IP address. You must set both before sharing files for the first time.

IP Address

To give a Windows computer an IP address:

1. If necessary, open the Network control panel and click on the Configuration tab.
2. Highlight the TCP/IP protocol in the list of installed network components.
3. Click the Properties button.
4. If you computer is not connected directly to the Internet, click the Specify an IP address radio button and enter the IP address and subnet mask, as in Figure 9-8. The only requirement for the IP address in this case is that it be different from that of any other computer on the network. However, if your computer is directly connected to the Internet, check with your network administrator or ISP to determine how the IP address and subnet mask should be set.
5. Click the OK button to save the settings.

Name and Workgroup

To give the computer a network identity:

1. If necessary, open the Network control panel and click the Identification tab.
2. Enter a computer name, workgroup, and description, as in Figure 9-9. The workgroup name should be the same as that of all other workstations in the same group.
3. Click the OK button to save the settings.

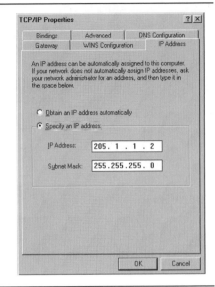

Figure 9-8:   Setting the IP address

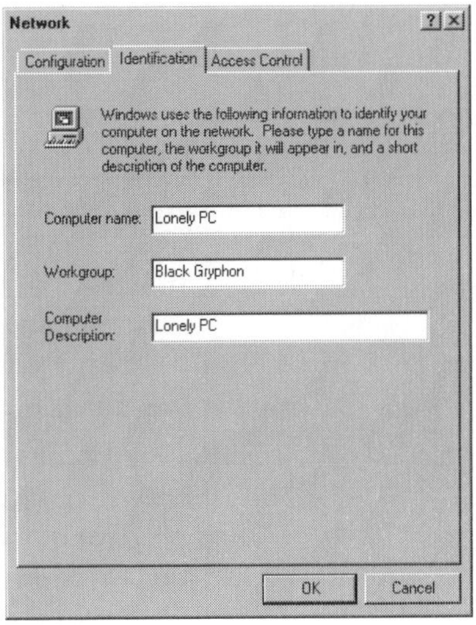

Figure 9-9:   Setting an owner name and password

Enable File Sharing

To enable file sharing:

1. Click on the Access Control tab in the Network control panel.

2. If it is not already highlighted, click the Share-level access control radio button, as in Figure 9-10.

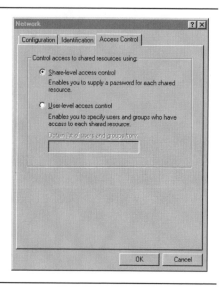

Figure 9-10:   Enabling file sharing

3. Click the OK button to save the settings.

4. Restart the computer.

5. When it restarts, you will be asked for a user name and password. Enter the user name for the owner of the computer and a password. (Just press Enter for no password.) Type the password again to confirm it. (Again, press Enter for no password.) Each time you start the computer after this, Windows will ask for the user name and password.

The purpose of the owner name and password, of course, is to give you control over who has access to your machine. Only someone with that owner name and password pair can change the file sharing settings on the computer.

Also keep in mind that Share-level access control allows you to set a password for each item that you share. However, all users who share that item must be given that same password. Given that the chance of a password becoming compromised goes up with the square of the number of people who know it, this is clearly not as secure as providing each remote user with his or her own user name and password.

Choosing Items to Be Shared and Setting Access Rights

Once you have enabled file sharing and rebooted with an owner name and password, you can choose items to be shared at any time. To make a disk or portion of a disk available to remote users:

1. Right-click on the disk or directory that you want to share.
2. Choose Sharing from the popup menu. The External Properties window appears.
3. If necessary, click on the Sharing tab.
4. Click the Share As radio button (see Figure 9-11).
5. Enter a name for the shared item in the Share Name box.
6. Click a radio button in the Access Type area to determine the type of access you want to give remote users.
7. If you want to require users to supply a password for a particular type of access, enter that password in the Passwords section. Note that the password boxes become available as the associated Access Type radio buttons are highlighted.
8. Click the OK button to save the settings.

Repeat this process for any disks or directories you want to share, including removable media such as CD-ROMs or Zip disks. To share printers, open the Printers folder in the Control Panel folder and right-click on the icon of the printer you want to share. Choose sharing from the pop-up menu and give it a shared name and password (if desired).

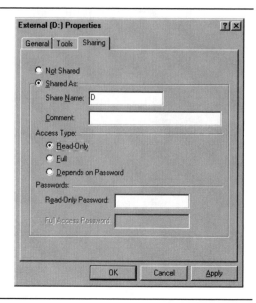

Figure 9-11:   Setting sharing properties

Connecting to Shared Resources

The procedures to connect to shared disks and printers are slightly different because shared printers must be added to a computer's list of printers.

Connecting to Shared Disks

A user who wants to mount disks or directories you have shared needs to do the following:

1.   Open Windows Explorer.
2.   Choose Map Network Drive from the Tools menu.
3.   Enter a drive letter to use for the network resource and the path to the drive (see Figure 9-12).

The path to a network drive is specified in the format:

\\computer_name\directory_name

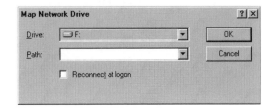

Figure 9-12: Mapping a network drive to a local drive letter

Once the drive has been mapped, the user can work with it as if it were a local drive, subject to the access rights established by the computer owner.

To disconnect from the network drive, the user returns to Windows Explorer and chooses Disconnect Network Drive from the Tools menu.

Connecting to Shared Printers

To connect to a shared printer, a user must do the following:

1. Open the Printers folder in the Control Panel folder.
2. Run the Add Printer wizard.
3. Choose Network as the type of printer to add (see Figure 9-13).

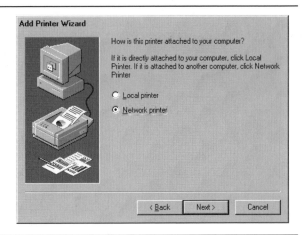

Figure 9-13: Indicating that a network printer is to be added

4.   Enter the path to the printer in the format

\\computer_name\share_name

as in Figure 9-14.

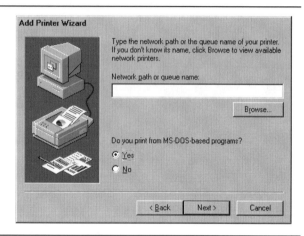

Figure 9-14:   Identifying a network printer

5.   Choose the manufacturer and model of the printer (see Figure 9-15).

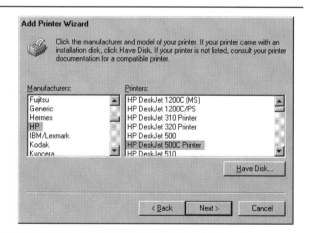

Figure 9-15:   Choosing the manufacturer and printer model of a network printer

6. Windows will copy the necessary driver files to the hard disk. If necessary, provide the Windows install disk containing the files.

Windows then creates a printer icon for the network printer. The user can work with it like any other printer connected directly to the user's computer.

Macintosh Operating System

The Macintosh OS supports peer-to-peer networking using the AppleShare protocol. A user who has been given access to all or part of a disk on another Macintosh on a network can mount the accessible disk on his or her desktop and use that disk as if it were a local volume. Hard disks and parts of hard disks may be shared. Removable media, such as CD-ROMs and Zip disks, can also be shared in this way.

> Note: Macintosh peer-to-peer networking does not need to support printer sharing. Sharing of printers connected directly to the network is provided by the AppleTalk software in every Macintosh. The capability to share printers connected to individual computers' serial ports is provided by specific printer drivers themselves.

Enabling File Sharing

To enable file sharing, the user whose Macintosh has the disks to be shared (the computer owner) must do at most six things:

- ♦ Establish a network identity. (Do this only once unless you need to make a change.)
- ♦ Choose EtherTalk networking. (Do this only once unless you need to make a change back to LocalTalk.)
- ♦ Create and activate a local TCP/IP configuration. (Do this only if necessary.)

♦ Set up user names and passwords for all users who will
  be allowed to share resources. (Do this only when necessary.)

♦ Turn on file sharing. (Do this each time you want to share
  disks.)

♦ Enable sharing for the specific disks to be shared if this
  has not been done previously. (Do this each time you
  want to share disks.)

Establishing a Network Identity

To establish a network identity, the computer owner opens the File
Sharing control panel (see Figure 9-16). He or she then enters the
owner name (the user name for the owner), a password, and a name
by which the computer will be known on the network in the top section of the window.

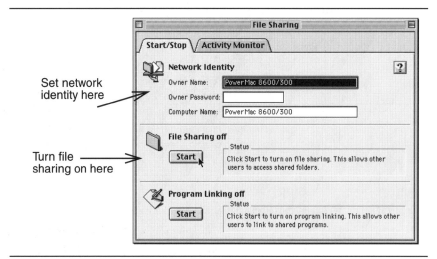

Figure 9-16: Setting a network identity

Choosing EtherTalk Networking

Switching from a Macintosh's built-in AppleTalk networking using
LocalTalk cabling to Ethernet is handled by the AppleTalk control
panel (Figure 9-17). Note that the precise options that appear in the

pop-up menu on this control panel depends on the model of Macintosh in use and whether Ethernet support is built into the motherboard or supplied on a NIC.

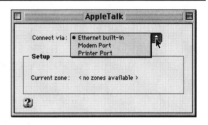

Figure 9-17:   Choosing EtherTalk

> *Note: When you add a NIC to a Macintosh, you install a software driver for the card. After that point, no further configuration is required. You simply choose the driver/NIC combination from the AppleTalk control panel to use that card.*

Creating and Activating a TCP/IP Configuration

The Macintosh OS supports multiple TCP/IP configurations, although only one can be active at a time. For example, if a computer uses TCP/IP to access the Internet through a modem and also uses TCP/IP for local networking, then there must be two separate configurations, one for each network.

To set up a new TCP/IP configuration, do the following:

1. Open the TCP/IP control panel.
2. Choose Configuration from the File menu (see Figure 9-18).
3. Select any existing configuration and click the Duplicate button.
4. Rename the new configuration.
5. Double-click on the new configuration to make it active and to gain access to it for editing, as in Figure 9-19.
6. Choose the network hardware to be used (for example, built-in AppleTalk, built-in Ethernet, or a NIC).

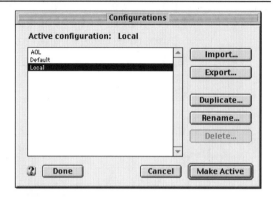

Figure 9-18:   Choosing a TCP/IP configuration

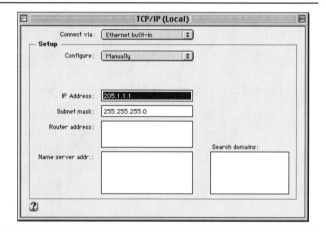

Figure 9-19:   Creating a TCP/IP configuration

7. Give the configuration an IP address and a subnet mask. As-
    suming that the network is not connected directly to the Inter-
    net, you can use the exact settings that appear in Figure 9-19. As
    mentioned earlier in this book, if the network is directly con-
    nected to the Internet, a network administrator or your ISP will
    let you know what the computer's IP address and subnet mask
    should be.

8. Close the TCP/IP control panel and save changes.

User Names and Passwords

User names and passwords are handled through the Users & Groups control panel (Figure 9-20). By default, each Macintosh has a user icon named Guest that controls access by people who are not registered users. A user icon with the same name as the computer's network identify represents the owner of the computer.

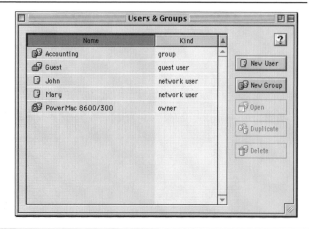

Figure 9-20: The Macintosh Users & Groups control panel

Note: The screen shots are of the Mac OS 8.1. File sharing is available with the 7.x versions, although the dialog boxes and some control panel names are different.

Each new user is given a name and a password (see Figure 9-21). The user is also given basic access rights, as in Figure 9-22. The user can be allowed to connect to the computer or to link to programs running on the computer.

Note: File linking became a part of the Macintosh OS with version 7.0. However, few programs support it and it is currently rarely used.

Users can be also assigned to groups to make it easier to give the same access rights to more than one user. For example, in Figure 9-22, the user named John is part of the Accounting group.

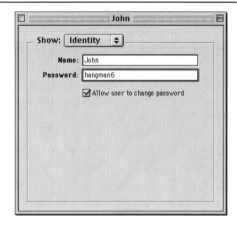

Figure 9-21:   Assigning a name and password to a user

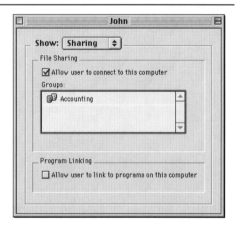

Figure 9-22:   Setting up basic file sharing rights

Turning on File Sharing

A Macintosh OS user turns on file sharing from the File Sharing control panel (Figure 9-16). The operating system enables file sharing for all mounted disk volumes that have previously been shared. If the owner of the computer wants to change which volumes are available for remote users, then it must be done *after* file sharing is enabled.

Sharing Specific Disks

Each mounted volume or folder on a volume can be given its own access control. To do so, the computer owner selects the object for which rights are to be assigned and chooses the Sharing command from the File menu. As you can see in Figure 9-23, the selected object can allow read/write, read only, write only, or no access to any specific user or group. The "Everyone" option applies to the Guest user and allows anyone to connect without a user name and password.

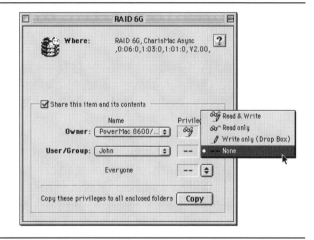

Figure 9-23:   Setting file sharing access rights

Mounting a Shared Disk

From the remote user's side, mounting a shared disk is no different from mounting an AppleShare volume. In fact, in many cases users will not recognize the difference between the two unless they are told.

To mount a remote volume, the user opens the Chooser, clicks on AppleShare, and selects a file server (Figure 9-24). The list at the top right of the window will include all AppleShare file servers as well as any computers that have enabled file sharing.

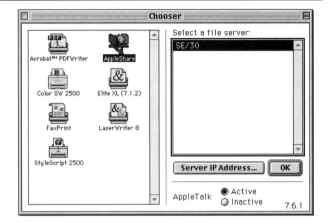

Figure 9-24:   Choosing a file server for mounting a shared volume

The remote user must then log in, either as a registered user or as a
guest (see Figure 9-25). Assuming that the login is successful, the
user chooses the available disk volumes that are to be mounted
from the volumes to which he or she has access (Figure 9-26). The
result is a new icon on the remote user's desktop that can be manip-
ulated and used like a local volume, within, of course, the restrictions imposed by the user's access rights. In Figure 9-27, for
example, the icon labeled SE/30 Hard Disk is a mounted network
volume.

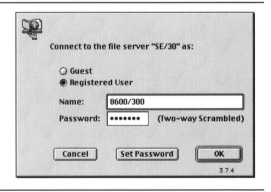

Figure 9-25:   Logging in to a shared volume

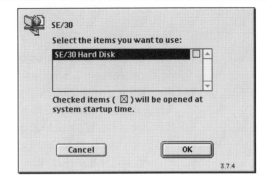

Figure 9-26:   Choosing a remote disk volume

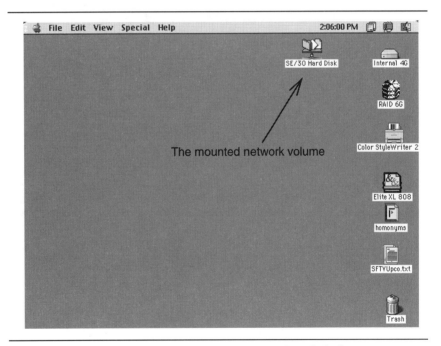

Figure 9-27:   A mounted network volume on a Macintosh desktop

Monitoring File Sharing Activity

The File Sharing control panel that a computer owner uses to start up file sharing can also be used to provide some simple monitoring of remote users who are connected at any given time. As you can see in Figure 9-28, the information a computer owner can gather is limited to which users and groups are connected, which local volumes are being shared, and the relative amount of network activity. Notice that it does *not* give any indication of which user is using which shared volume.

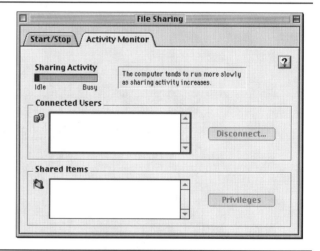

Figure 9-28:   Monitoring the activity of connected remote users

10

Integrating Multiple Operating Systems

Many of today's networks include client workstations that do not run the same operating system. One of the most common arrangements, for example, is a network with a Windows NT server and clients that run Windows 95, Windows 98, and the Macintosh OS. Alternatively, you may encounter a primarily Macintosh network with an AppleShare server that includes a few Windows machines.

In this chapter we will look at several ways to integrate workstations running different operating systems into the same network and how you can provide access to servers and other shared hardware from those workstations that have an OS different from that of the server. The basis of the solution is third-party software, some of which works from the Windows side and some from the Macintosh side.

179

Integrating Macintosh OS Computers into a Windows NT Network

If you have a few Macintosh OS computers on a predominantly Windows-based network, you can allow the Macintoshes to access your NT server and networked printers using a piece of commercial software from Thursby Software Systems called DAVE. DAVE allows Macintoshes to mount shared NT server volumes and to use them as if they were local Macintosh OS volumes. It also supports real-time message exchange between networked users and the sharing of network printers.

To use DAVE, a Macintosh user logs on to the network with a user name and password that has previously been established by a network administrator (see Figure 10-1). The user can then access any network resources to which the selected domain has access.

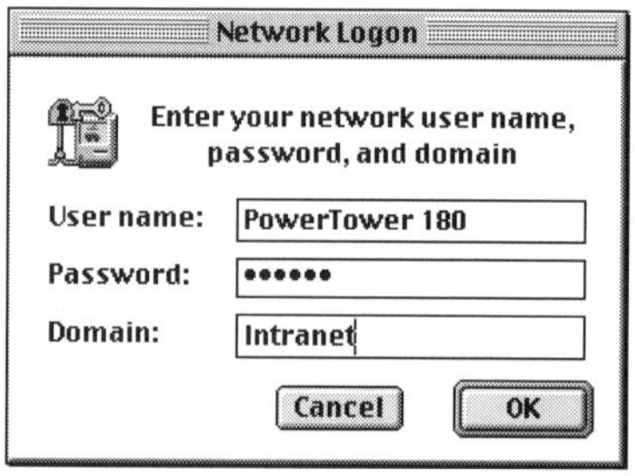

Figure 10-1:   Logging into an NT server using DAVE

While working with DAVE, the user can use a floating palette that contains the most commonly used network access commands (Figure 10-2): logging on and off, mounting volumes, sending messages to other users, and setting messaging preferences. This is a common metaphor used by Macintosh software and therefore makes working with DAVE comfortable for Macintosh OS users.

Figure 10-2:   The DAVE command palette

To mount a server volume, a user can either use the Chooser to select a server to mount a volume, just as he or she would mount an
AppleShare volume (see Figure 10-3), or mount the server manually, as in Figure 10-4.

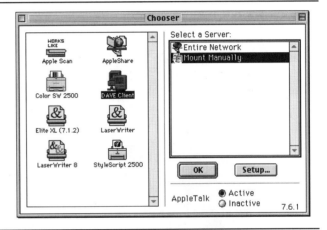

Figure 10-3:   Using the Macintosh Chooser to find an NT file server

Figure 10-4:   Using DAVE to mount a server volume manually

DAVE uses the NetBIOS protocol stack along with TCP/IP. It installs NetBIOS as a Macintosh system extension but also requires either TCP/IP or OpenTransport.

Integrating Windows Computers into a Macintosh Network

If your network is predominantly Macintosh, but you need to integrate a few Windows machines, then you can use the commercial add-on product PC MACLAN to provide an AppleTalk protocol stack for Windows. In addition to giving Windows machines access to AppleShare servers and shared AppleTalk printers, the software also allows Macintoshes on the network to mount Windows NT servers (see Figure 10-5).

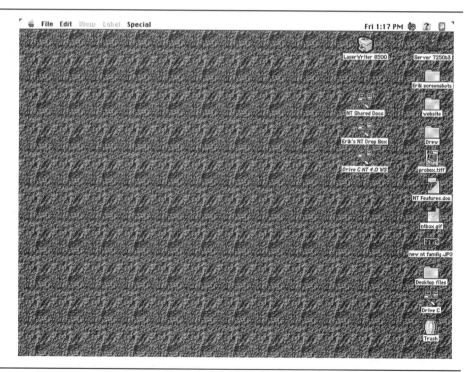

Figure 10-5:   NT server volumes mounted on a Macintosh desktop using PC MACLAN

PC MACLAN provides Windows machines with user and group access controls like those available with Mac OS peer-to-peer networking. As you can see in Figure 10-6, the process is identical to that of the Macintosh Users & Groups control panel described in Chapter 9.

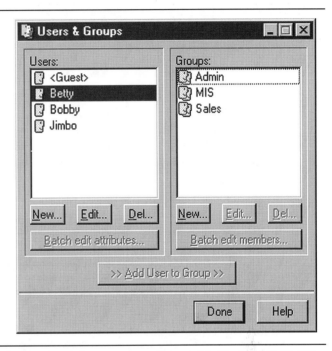

Figure 10-6: Windows users and groups security provided by PC MACLAN

Once user and group access has been established, PC MACLAN lets the Windows user identify which directories are to be shared, just as a Macintosh user would (see Figure 10-7).

PC MACLAN provides a Windows computer with an overview of an entire Macintosh network (Figure 10-8). It also gives Windows users access to AppleShare volumes and network printers available on the network, as in Figure 10-9.

> *Note: The major difference between DAVE and PC MACLAN is that DAVE works primarily from the Macintosh side and PC MACLAN works primarily from the Windows side.*

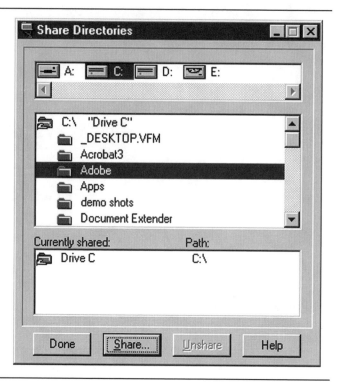

Figure 10-7: Using PC MACLAN to share Windows directories

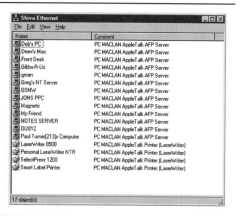

Figure 10-8: Viewing the zones in a Macintosh network from a Windows computer

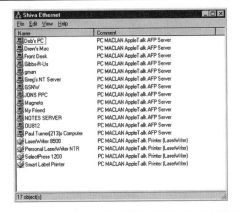

Figure 10-9: Viewing AppleShare volumes and networked printers from a Windows computer

Remote Control

In addition to giving mixed-platform network access to file server volumes, there is a class of software that provides multiplatform *remote control*. Such software allows a user on a network (or a user who has dialed into the network over a telephone line) to control or observe another computer. The software also supports file transfer and real-time chatting between users. To enable remote control, both computers must be running the remote control software.

A major use of remote control software is troubleshooting. When a user is having a system problem, a network administrator can observe what the user is doing from his or her workstation, without needing to physically go to the user's location. The network administrator can also control the remote user's computer to make changes to the system.

Users who are out of the office can also use remote control software to dial into their office machines from a laptop computer. This provides the remote user with access to the networked machine, and thus to the facilities of the network.

A widely used example of remote control software is Timbuktu Pro from Netopia (formerly Farallon). Available for Windows and Macintosh platforms, the software works almost identically from either side. The Windows version supports connections using TCP/IP and IPX; the Macintosh version supports AppleTalk and TCP/IP. Both versions also support connections through a modem connected directly to the computer.

> *Note: If you have a Windows-only network, an alternative to Timbuktu Pro is PC Anywhere.*

To allow other users access to his or her computer, a Timbuktu Pro user first configures remote user permissions. As you can see in Figure 10-10, each remote user can be given a name and password along with user-specific access rights. In this case, the rights are an "all or nothing" affair: Either a remote user can or cannot perform an action.

Figure 10-10:   Configuring a Timbuktu Pro user

Making a Connection

Timbuktu Pro is loaded into main memory at system start-up and runs in the background until a user needs to use it to access a remote computer. Regardless of what a remote user wants to do with a networked computer, he or she must first establish a connection with that machine. For a TCP/IP connection, the remote user must know the TCP/IP address of the computer, as in Figure 10-11 (Windows) and Figure 10-12 (Macintosh), or the network name of the computer if your network is running Domain Name Services (DNS). When working with AppleTalk, Timbuktu Pro is also able to provide a list of computers that are also running the software (see Figure 10-13).

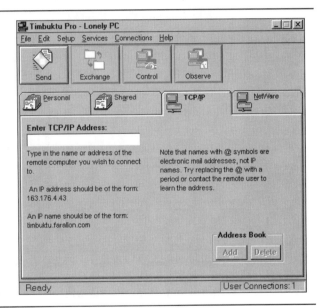

Figure 10-11:   Opening a new TCP/IP connection from a Windows PC

Observation and Control

When a remote user is observing or controlling another computer on the network, the screen of the computer to which the remote user is connected appears in a window on the remote user's monitor. For example, in Figure 10-14 you can see a portion of the start-up monitor

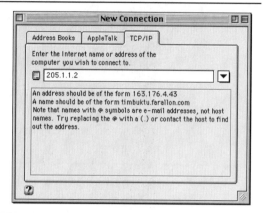

Figure 10-12:   Opening a new TCP/IP connection from a Macintosh

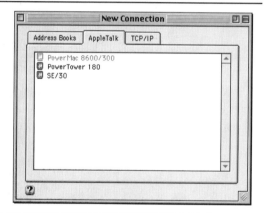

Figure 10-13:   Opening a new AppleTalk connection

of a Macintosh appearing in a window on a Windows 95 desktop.
You can find the opposite—a Windows 95 monitor in a Macintosh
window—in Figure 10-15.

If observing, the remote user sees everything that occurs on the remote screen, but has no control over that computer. If controlling,
whenever the remote user's mouse pointer is over the remote window, the actions affected the remote computer, allowing the remote
user to do anything his or her access rights allow with that remote
machine.

Figure 10-14:   A Macintosh screen in a Timbuktu Pro window on a Windows PC

Note: If a Macintosh has multiple monitors, then Timbuktu Pro shows only the start-up monitor, that is, the one containing the menu bar.

File Exchange

Timbuktu supports two types of file exchange, which it calls "sending" files and "exchanging" files. Sending a file transfers it to a single drop folder on the remote computer. Exchanging files gives the remote user complete control over where transferred files are placed, as in Figure 10-16. The interface for exchanging files from a Windows machine is identical to the Macintosh interface.

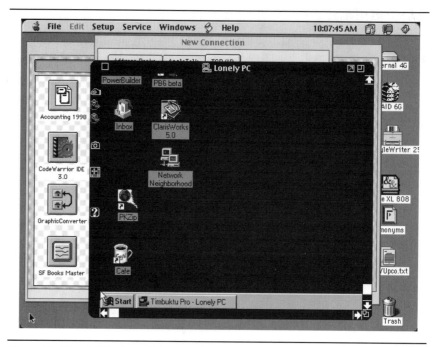

Figure 10-15:   A Windows 95 screen in a Timbuktu Pro window on a Macintosh

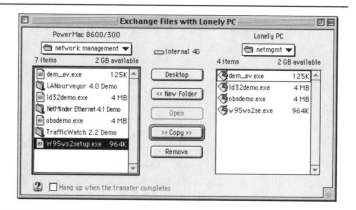

Figure 10-16:   Using Timbuktu Pro to exchange files

Messaging

Timbuktu Pro provides two ways for users to exchange real-time messages. The first is through a relatively standard chat room interface, such as that in Figure 10-17. A user can add himself or herself to a chat session, or a user can add a remote computer to a chat session (assuming that the remote user has the access rights to do so).

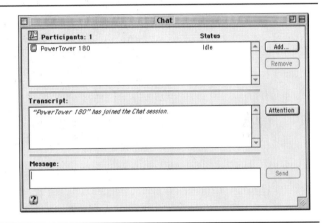

Figure 10-17:   Timbuktu Pro chat

If networked computers are equipped with microphones and speakers, Timbuktu Pro provides an intercom service that allows users to speak with each other (see Figure 10-18). This can provide an alternative to a long-distance phone call when the remote user has dialed in to the network from some other location, perhaps using a dedicated line. (If the remote user is paying long-distance charges to connect to the network, there of course would be no savings.)

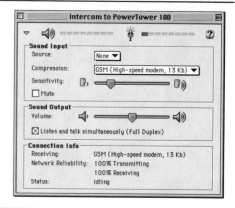

Figure 10-18:   Establishing a Timbuktu Pro intercom session

11

Network Monitoring and Discovery

Once you have your network up and running, you will probably want to monitor the traffic patterns on that network. Such monitoring can, for example, help you identify network segments that are under- or overloaded. With that information in hand, you may decide to reconfigure the network to balance the traffic more evenly. Network monitoring can also help you find problems, including network devices that have gone down or are no longer accessible.

Network monitoring (often referred to as "network management") can be performed with any of a wide range of software packages. In this chapter you will be introduced to a sampling of those packages and the capabilities they provide.

True network management is a lot more than simply collecting network traffic statistics and monitoring performance. It involves troubleshooting, user support, upgrade planning, perfor-

mance tuning, and so on. Therefore, although much of this software is marketed as "network management" software, it certainly does not provide all the management a network requires.

Network monitoring software can also be used for *network discovery,* a process through which software traverses the network to discover its layout. This is of particular use when you inherit the management of a network that has grown without planning and you do not really know what devices are connected or how the network is configured. As you will see, some of the products discussed in this chapter can also be used for that purpose.

> *Note: Most of the screen shots in this chapter were taken from demonstration software provided free by the software developers. Typically, a demo version is fully functional but limited either in the amount of time for which it will work (for example, 30 days) or in the number of times you can launch the program. Most of these demos can be downloaded from the companies' web sites, making it easy for you to test these packages before you decide which one you want to purchase. See Appendix B for contact information.*

Windows-Only Networks

There are many choices for networking monitoring if your network consists of only Windows computers (95, 98, NT). What you will find in this section is a sampling of products that provide a wide range of network monitoring information.

LANdecoder

The following types of data about a network are among the real-time outputs of LANdecoder (from Triticom).

- ◆ Which devices are communicating with each other, including the number of packets exchanged and the error rate during that exchange (Figure 11-1). Such data are useful for identifying high-traffic devices and for troubleshooting areas of the network that are susceptible to high error rates.

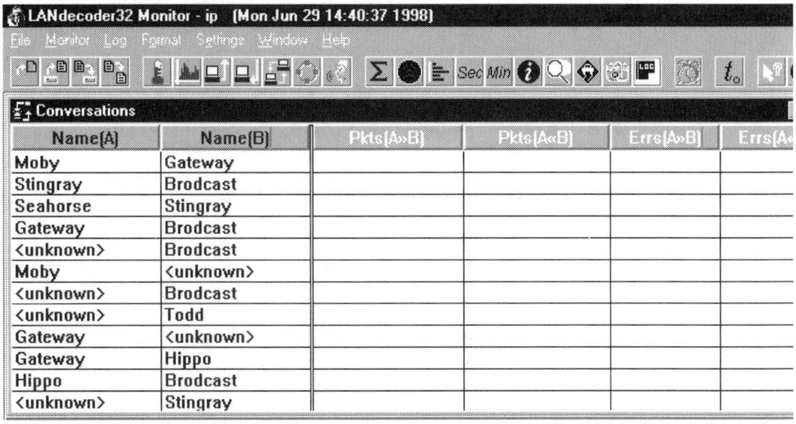

Name[A]	Name[B]	Pkts[A»B]	Pkts[A«B]	Errs[A»B]	Errs[A«
Moby	Gateway				
Stingray	Brodcast				
Seahorse	Stingray				
Gateway	Brodcast				
<unknown>	Brodcast				
Moby	<unknown>				
<unknown>	Brodcast				
<unknown>	Todd				
Gateway	<unknown>				
Gateway	Hippo				
Hippo	Brodcast				
<unknown>	Stingray				

Figure 11-1: LANdecoder conversation display

♦ The distribution of the size of packets on the network (Figure 11-2). These data are likewise useful for identifying high-traffic devices that might, for example, need to upgraded from 10BASE-T to 100BASE-T to relieve a performance bottleneck.

♦ The percentage of network bandwidth being used over time (Figure 11-3). With these data, you can identify times of day when the network is heavily loaded and, if necessary, institute upgrades or procedures that will help balance peak loads.

♦ An overview of network usage and performance ("vital signs" in Figure 11-4). The dials represent network utilization, number of frames sent, number of octets (groups of eight bits) sent, error rate, the amount of bandwidth being used, and the rate of multicast packets sent.

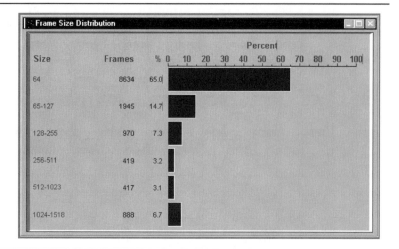

Figure 11-2:   LANdecoder packet size distribution display

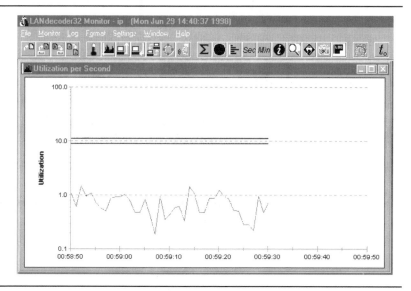

Figure 11-3:   LANdecoder network utilization graph

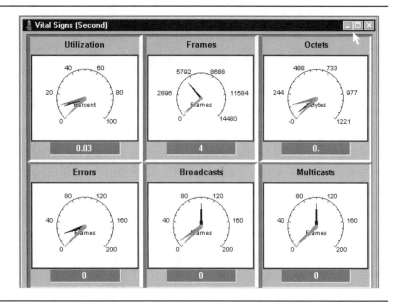

Figure 11-4:: LANdecoder network vital signs display

Network Observer

Network Observer provides its displays in the right side of its main window. The toolbar allows the displays to be viewed as text, graphs, or dials. Among the types of data it displays are the following:

♦ Network utilization (Figure 11-5), graphing the load on the overall network.

♦ Collision analysis (Figure 11-6), providing the number of collisions that occur when devices attempt to access the network media. The display also indicates devices that encounter an "excessive" number of collisions. Any devices so identified—assuming the excessive collisions occur throughout the workday rather than just at peak load times—are candidates for either movement to a less heavily used network segment or for upgrading to a faster type of Ethernet.

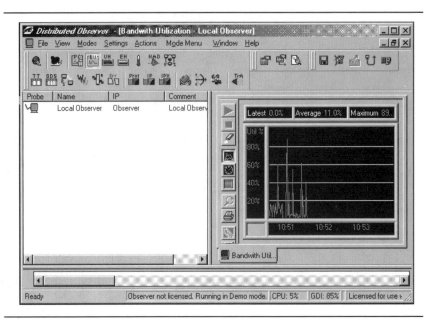

Figure 11-5:   Network Observer network utilization display

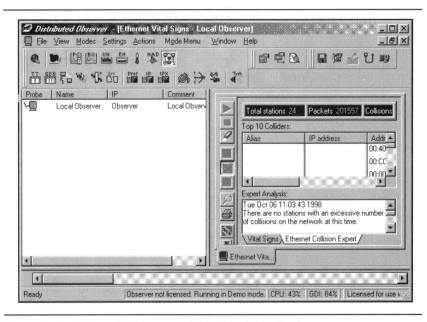

Figure 11-6:   Network Observer collision analysis display

♦ Network trends display (Figure 11-7), which summarizes the number devices on the network, the number of packets exchanged, and the volume of data exchanged. By restarting data collection at various times throughout the workday, a network administrator can collect information about how network loads vary with time.

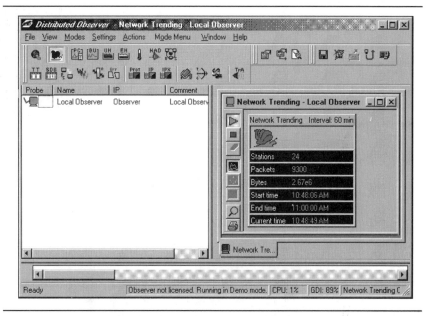

Figure 11-7: Network Observer network trends display

♦ Packets captured (Figure 11-8), a graph of the distribution of the size of packets actually received by devices on the network. Packets that were "dropped" (somehow never delivered to their destination) are also graphed. In this particular example, there are no dropped packets, so the "dropped" line appears only at the bottom of the graph.

♦ A vital signs display (Figure 11-9), providing an overview of network traffic, including the amount of data sent over time and the result of CRC (cyclical redundancy checking) error verifications. As with LANdecoder's vital signs display, the purpose of this graph is to give the network administrator a quick overview of network loading and performance.

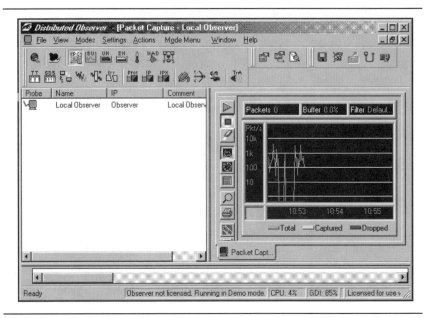

Figure 11-8: Network Observer packets captured display

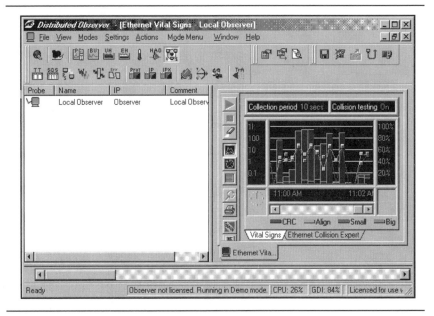

Figure 11-9: Network Observer vital signs display

Mixed OS Networks

The choices for networks that include Macintosh, Windows, and UNIX computers are more limited than those for Windows-only networks. One suite of products that provides network monitoring for both the AppleTalk and TCP/IP protocols includes the LANsurveyor and TrafficWatch programs.

As you can see in Figure 11-10, LANsurveyor provides a map of all devices on a network segment at any given time. It works by actually scanning the network for all devices running a selected protocol. In this particular example, the protocol stack is AppleTalk; the product works identically with TCP/IP, providing a map for networks of any operating system running that protocol stack. If a device does not appear as you would expect, then you know that the device is not working properly.

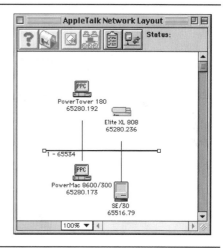

Figure 11-10:   A LANsurveyor network map

TrafficWatch provides a real-time monitor of network activity. In Figure 11-11, you can see the device list produced by scanning the network. In this context, a "device" is anything (hardware or software) that uses a network protocol to communicate. For example, the second physical device (the PowerTower 180), shows up as both an AppleShare server and a Timbuktu Pro host because each software package uses part of the AppleTalk protocol stack. A device list of this type provides a network administrator with information about which software is currently running. If something is missing, or something unauthorized is present, the network administrator can take the actions necessary to correct the problem.

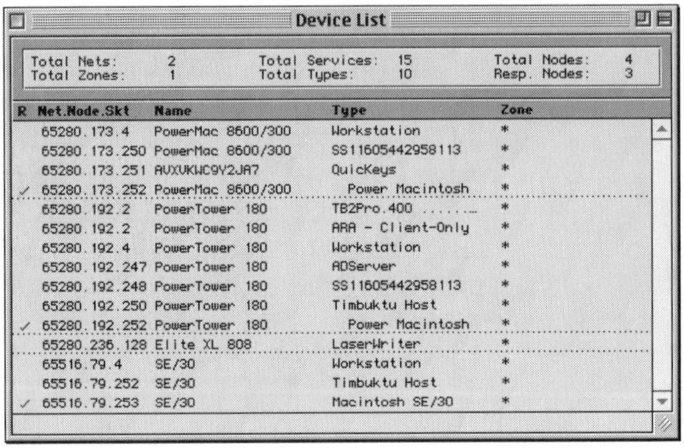

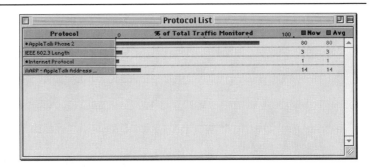

Figure 11-11:   TrafficWatch device list display

The protocol list display in Figure 11-12 indicates the proportion of traffic on the network using specific protocols. In this particular example, which was based on network devices using AppleTalk, there is actually some IP traffic as well.

Figure 11-12:   TrafficWatch protocol use display

The traffic list display (for example, Figure 11-13) shows the percentage distribution of network traffic by network device. The example in Figure 11-13 represents packets sent between a workstation and a printer. This information can help identify devices that heavily load the network and that might benefit by being isolated into separate network segments.

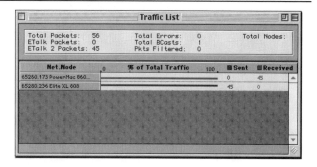

Figure 11-13:   TrafficWatch traffic list display

The network utilization display (for example, Figure 11-14) provides a graph of the load on the network over time. It can help a network administrator identify heavy use periods. It can also demonstrate whether the current network bandwidth is sufficient to handle traffic under peak loads.

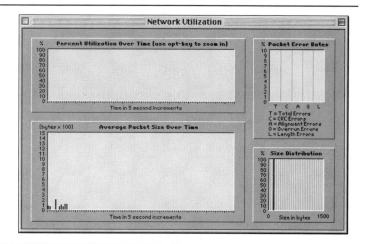

Figure 11-14:   TrafficWatch network utilization display

Part Four

Ethernet Solution Examples

In this final part of the book you will read about the Ethernet networks designed for three businesses: a small real estate office, a medium-size law firm, and a large insurance company. These fictional organizations will illustrate many of the concepts discussed throughout this book and give you a perspective on how network solutions change with the size of the company. In addition, you will see some of the factors that influence the decisions that a network designer might make.

> Note: The designs for the networks that you see in this part of the book are definitely the author's opinion on how the networks should be configured. Feel free to disagree! The point is for you to understand why the decisions were made as much as to show you specific solutions.

First, however, you will be introduced to network design software, programs that can help you configure and document network designs. Such software also can simulate, using animation, traffic on a network.

12

Network Design and Simulation Software

As you read in Chapter 11, many of today's LANs have grown without overall planning. When it is unclear how a network is configured, network discovery software provides a way for a network administrator to map the hardware and software on his or her network. If, however, you have the luxury of being able to plan an entire network *before* it is implemented—as you might if your company was moving to a new location—then you can take advantage of some powerful software to help you do so. Such network design and simulation software can also let you test the network under different traffic loads and under a variety of failure conditions.

Network design and simulation software typically provides the following capabilities:

- Modeling of many size networks, from global to within a single floor
- Tools for diagramming the physical layout of a network, including the ability to place vendor-specific hardware and software
- The ability to layer network diagrams, collapsing and expanding smaller units, such as a wiring closet, within a larger unit (for example, a floor)
- Storage for customized network configuration documentation, including quotes from vendors, equipment speeds, and so on
- The ability to specify traffic loads through specific nodes on the network and to use animation to simulate the performance of the network under those assumptions.
- The ability to simulate failures of any network device and view animated simulations of how routers and switches can reroute traffic.

In addition, network simulations can help identify potential design trouble spots, such as loops or cascades that are too long.

The software that will be used for examples in this chapter is Net-Cracker Designer from NetCracker Technology. It runs in Windows 95, Windows 98, and Windows NT, and is typical of high-end network design and simulation software.

> *Note: To the best of this author's knowledge, there is no network design and simulation software available for the Macintosh. A message posted to the Evangelist generated nothing but messages suggesting network monitoring and discovery software along with messages from people looking for the very same thing.*

Network Design Tools

At its heart, network design software is a specialized drawing program. Most such programs let you arrange icons for hardware and software and then link those icons into a network. You may also find that you can nest larger objects, such as floors within a building, expanding them as needed to see the network detail within a containing object.

The Network Hierarchy

Most business networks involve more than one room and often more than a single floor. To help you organize a network design based on a hierarchy of physical subunits, network design software usually provides objects—known as *containers* with NetCracker Designer—that can be collapsed within one another. This nesting can greatly simplify the design of a large network. It can also help manage such a network by providing a variety of levels at which the network's configuration can be viewed.

The network that will be used to demonstrate the use of a diagramming and simulation tool is contained in several rooms on a single floor. As you can see in Figure 12-1, an icon for the floor appears in a window named "Top," indicating that it is the top level in the network. The small rectangle drawn around the icon indicates that it is a container and that it can be expanded to show detail. The tree structure at the left of the window shows the overall container hierarchy.

> *Note: Given that this network occupies only one floor, it is not strictly necessary to include an icon for the floor. However, if the network ever expands beyond a single floor, creating the diagram in this way will make diagramming the expansion much easier.*

When expanded, the floor icon provides a window for the contents of the floor (Figure 12-2). Although it may be difficult to see in the illustration, each of the icons in Figure 12-2 is surrounded by a boundary rectangle, indicating that all of them are also containers.

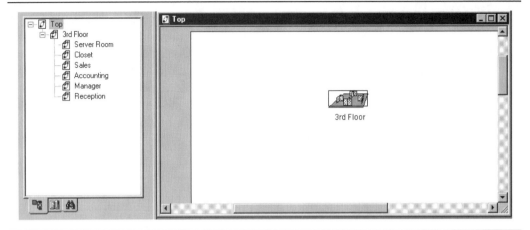

Figure 12-1:   The top level of the sample network

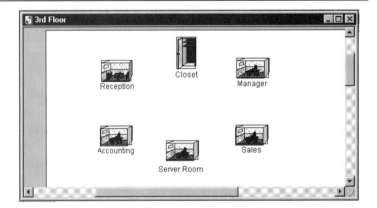

Figure 12-2:   The expanded floor container, displaying five rooms and a wiring closet

Choosing and Configuring Network Devices

In Figure 12-3 you can see the NetCracker Designer work area. The scrolling list at the left of the window contains categories of network hardware and software. The icons available within a category appear in the icon well at the bottom of the window. You can drag icons from the well into the work area to add them to the network.

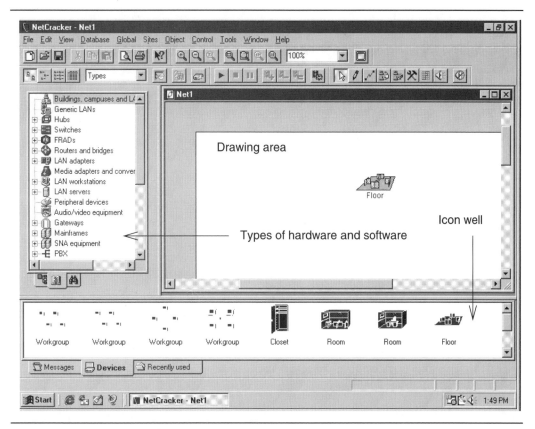

Figure 12-3: The NetCracker Designer work area

Icons for network devices and software can be generic, as they appear in Figure 12-4. Alternatively, you can choose from a database of specific devices. For example, in Figure 12-5, the icon well contains hubs from 3Com's SuperStack line.

If you cannot find an icon in the program's database that matches the hardware or software you need, you can custom-configure your own devices, which are then stored in a user database for use wherever needed. (You will read more about this shortly.)

Device Properties

The device icons serve multiple purposes. Not only do they indicate network devices in a graphic representation of the network layout,

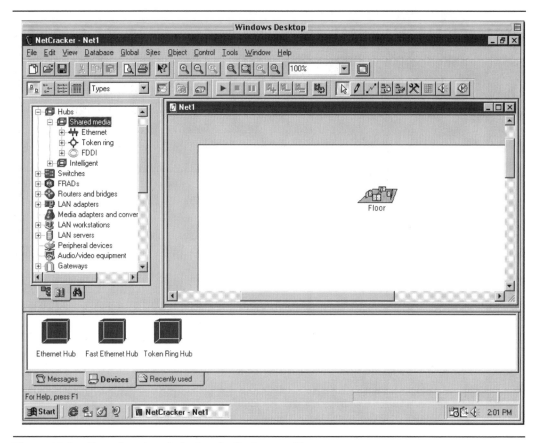

Figure 12-4:   Generic network devices in the icon well

but they can be used to document a great deal of information about each device. For example, in Figure 12-6 you can see the General properties for a stackable hub. This particular panel provides information such as the manufacturer, model number, and catalog number of the device.

Specific purchase quotes can be stored in the Price/Support Properties panel (Figure 12-7). As you can see, this makes it possible to store complete information about a device along with the network layout diagram.

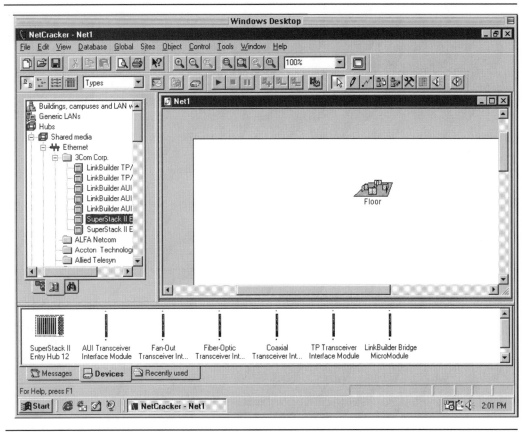

Figure 12-5   Vendor-specific devices in the icon well

Perhaps the most important parts of a network device are its ports. Device properties therefore include a separate listing of all ports supplied with or added to a device, as in Figure 12-8. Each port can then be configured individually (see Figure 12-9).

Custom-built Icons

NetCracker's Device Factory lets you create devices that do not appear in the database. For example, NetCracker 1.5, the version from which the examples in this chapter were taken, did not include any Gigabit Ethernet NICs. However, the network needed those devices in its servers.

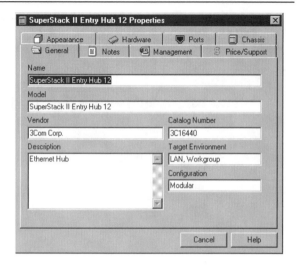

Figure 12-6: General device properties

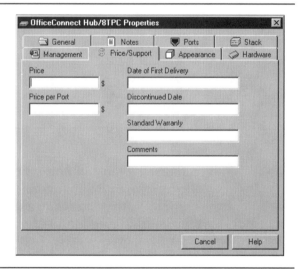

Figure 12-7: Price/support properties

The Device Factory is actually a Windows Wizard that takes you through the process of configuring a new device. For the Gigabit Ethernet NIC, you would begin by choosing the type of device (Figure 12-10) and then giving the custom device a name (Figure 12-11).

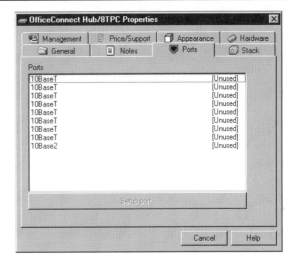

Figure 12-8: Device port list

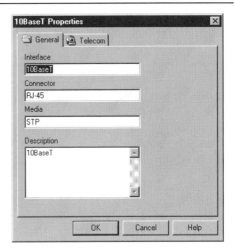

Figure 12-9: Port properties

This name will be used to identify the device in a database of user-created devices. The new device can therefore be used as often as needed in the network design.

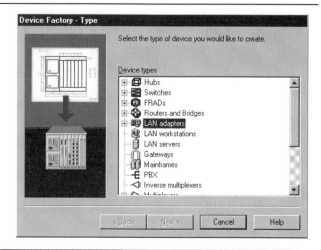

Figure 12-10:   Choosing the general type for a custom device

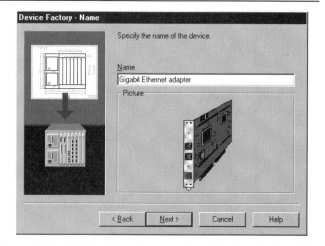

Figure 12-11:   Giving a custom device a name

What happens after a device is named depends on the type of device. In the case of a NIC, the only other configuration necessary is the type of bus in which the card will fit (see Figure 12-12). If, however, you are creating a PC or workstation, you will need to specify ports, hard drives, removable media drives, RAM, and so on.

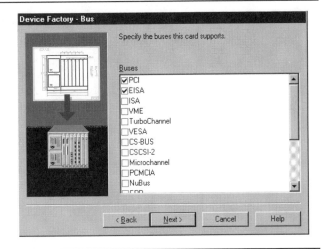

Figure 12-12:   Choosing bus types for a custom NIC

Linking Network Devices

To establish links between network devices, you click on a pair of devices to be linked with a linking tool. If the two devices are within the same container, then the process is simple: You click twice and then configure the link. However, if the two devices are in different locations—such as a workstation in a specific room and a switch in a wiring closet—then linking is a four-step process:

1. Click on the containers in which the devices to be linked are found. The software draws a dashed line between the containers to indicate that there is an incomplete link (Figure 12-13).

2. Open one of the containers. You will see a small square that represents the link. Click on the square and the device being linked with the linking tool. Because the link is still incomplete, the line between the square and the device is dashed (Figure 12-14).

3. Open the second container. Click on the square representing the link and the device being linked with the linking tool.

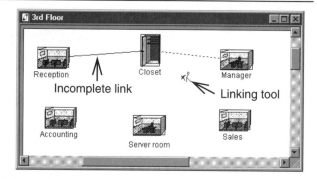

Figure 12-13:   Linking containers

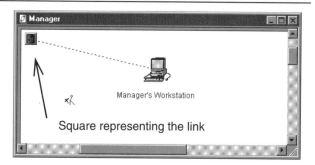

Figure 12-14:   Setting the first half of the link

4. The Link Assistant dialog box appears (Figure 12-15). The soft-
    ware chooses a pair of compatible ports for the link. If there are
    other compatible ports, you can change the selection. Then you
    click the Link button and close the dialog box. Because the link
    is complete, all lines representing the link are now solid, as in
    Figure 12-16.

The colors of the link lines represent the type of media. Although
this book is printed in black and white, you may be able to tell that
one of the lines in Figure 12-17 is lighter than the others. This is the
fiber optic link to a Gigabit/Fast Ethernet switch in the server room.
(The switch has Gigabit Ethernet ports for the servers and a Fast
Ethernet port to connect to the switch in the wiring closet.) The remainder of the links are blue, indicating UTP wiring.

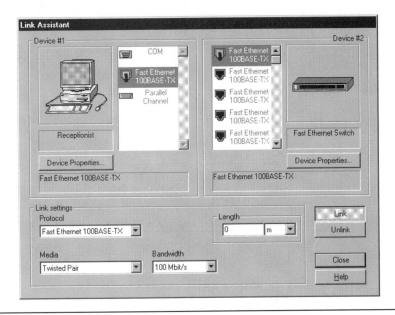

Figure 12-15:   Configuring a link

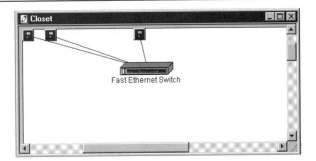

Figure 12-16:   Completed links

Although this particular software does not allow you to customize a label for the square representing the links, each square contains a small icon of the type of device to which the link is connected. For example, in Figure 12-17 the link to the switch in the server room has what appears to be a thick line in it; this is actually a tiny drawing of a switch. The remaining squares have small PCs in them be-

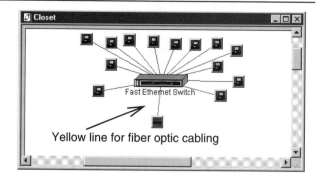

Figure 12-17:   Completed links to switch in wiring closet

cause each link goes directly to a PC. In addition, holding the mouse pointer briefly over a square brings up a hot tip with the name of the device and its container.

Simulating Network Traffic

One of the most useful things network design software can do for you is to simulate network traffic using animation so that you can identify potential problems. For example, a traffic simulation can help you identify bottlenecks that slow up traffic, indicating that you perhaps need to further segment your network.

Assigning Traffic Loads

To be able to simulate network traffic, software needs to know the type of traffic that will be traveling between any two devices. The number of packets that travel between any two workstations, for example, will generally be far less than traffic between a database server and a workstation.

Before you can animate traffic, you must therefore set up traffic flows. Using Netcracker Designer you click on the two devices that will be communicating with the set traffic tool. Then, you assign a traffic profile, as in Figure 12-18.

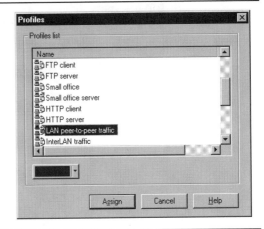

Figure 12-18:   Assigning a traffic profile

Each of the preconfigured traffic profiles represents a typical conversation of a given type. For example, peer-to-peer traffic will be
more sporadic than workstation-to-database server traffic. It is
therefore probably a major understatement to say that the useful-
ness of a simulation rests in appropriate choices for the traffic profiles! It is also true that you are relying on the developer of the
software to provide realistic estimates of the characteristics of network traffic. Only your knowledge of your own network traffic
loads (or estimated loads, if you are designing a new network) and
experience with a given network simulation product can determine
how closely a simulation matches what occurs in the actual network.

> *Note: An enhanced version of this product — NetCracker
> Professional — lets you create your own traffic profiles.*

The colored rectangle in the lower left of the dialog box sets the col-
or with which the flow of packets will be illustrated. While the animation is running, the color is assigned to a small shape that
indicates the protocol in use. In the example you will see, all the
packets are rectangular, indicating that they are TCP/IP packets.

Packet characteristics for the entire network are configured separately. As you can see in Figure 12-19, the sliders provide relative settings

for intensity (the rate at which packets are generated), speed (the speed at which an individual packet travels), and packet size.

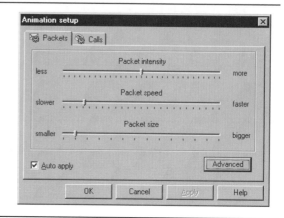

Figure 12-19:   Configuring packets for animation

Running Simulations

After assigning traffic flows, you simply start the animation. The animation appears in all windows that contain data flows, and you can switch between windows to view the traffic at various levels in the network hierarchy.

As an example, in Figure 12-20 you can see the data flow between a workstation and a printer. Although the two devices are located in the same room, the network connection between them is in the wiring closet. That is why the flow is not connected directly. This is one drawback to using containers to organize a network: Viewing the contents of a container does not necessary indicate how two devices within the container are connected.

If you move to the window showing the entire floor, however, there is both more and less information (Figure 12-21). It is clear that there is traffic between the Sales, Reception, and Manager's offices, but exactly which devices are communicating is not clear.

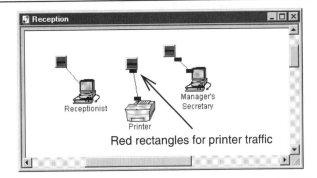

Figure 12-20: **Traffic flow between a workstation and a network printer**

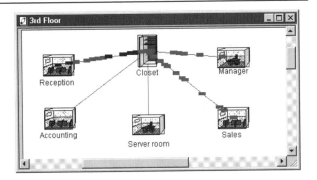

Figure 12-21: **Traffic flow within an entire floor**

One of the reasons the animation gives less information than we might like is the design of this network. Because the network is very small (only about 15 nodes), all workstations are connected to the same switch in the wiring closet. However, if each room was a workgroup with its own hub, which in turn was connected to a switch in the wiring closet, then the animation would be able to show traffic flows through each hub, providing a more complete view of peer-to-peer traffic. As you will see as you read through the network design examples in the following chapters, network animation becomes more effective with larger networks.

> *Note: It goes without saying that you should not design your network around the animation provided by network design software.*

Documenting the Network Design

As you read earlier, network design software allows you to store information that you can use to document network device purchasing plans. Network design software therefore provides a variety of reports that include information stored in device configuration/properties dialog boxes.

NetCracker Designer, for example, provides the preconfigured reports in Figure 12-22. The summaries can be generated for any level in the hierarchy or for the entire network. Reports can include sublevels in the hierarchy and provide grouping by container.

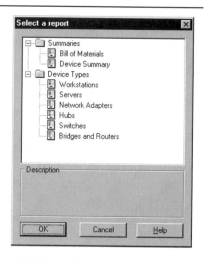

Figure 12-22:   Available reports

As an example, take a look at the partial Device Summary report that appears in Figure 12-23. This report lists each device along with its manufacturer and model. For a "shopping list" of network components, you would use the Bill of Materials report. The reports grouped by device type provide shopping lists for specific categories of hardware.

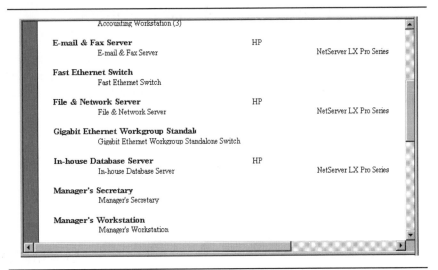

Figure 12-23:   A portion of the Device Summary report, showing device, manufacturer, and model

As you might imagine, the reports are only as complete as the information entered into the network design. If a designer does not bother to include vendor and price information in the device properties, then that data will not show up in the reports.

13

Ethernet Example 1: Small-But-Growing Real Estate

Small-But-Growing Real Estate (SBG) is an independent real estate brokerage that represents both buyers and sellers of homes and property. Established in 1985, the business is run as a sole proprietorship by Gregory Banks. In this chapter you will read about the introduction of a new network into an established, very small business. The choices that the business makes are not only related to its size and current needs, but also to the potential for further growth.

Business Overview

Mr. Banks originally worked alone from his home. In 1989 he hired his first employee (another certified real estate broker). By 1992, he had three employees (another broker and a clerical assistant), at which point he moved from his home to his current storefront location.

Today, SBG employs six brokers and two clerical assistants. Each clerical assistant is equipped with a stand-alone PC that is used primarily for word processing. The office also has two workstations that are connected by a POTS line to a multiple-listing service and a PC used for e-mail. All five computers have their own dot-matrix printers.

The only Internet access at this time is a dial-up connection from the e-mail computer. Employees must physically go to the computer to sign on to their e-mail accounts (hosted by a local ISP), receive e-mail, and respond to it.

Network Plans and Design

As the next step in promoting his business, Mr. Banks would like to give his business an Internet presence. He has seen the web sites prepared by other real estate offices and believes that the sales of items listed through his office would increase significantly if he could reach the wide audience of the Internet. After talking with a computer consultant, Mr. Banks realizes that there was a lot more to an Internet presence than some fancy graphics. He knows that the time has come to put a networked PC at each employee's desk. The clerical assistants will get new desktops; the brokers will get laptops that they can take into the field. Mr. Banks also wants to add a single, networked printer.

The brokers will be trained to use digital cameras and to upload photos of newly listed properties to a file server, where they can be accessed by the part-time employee who will be designing and maintaining the web site. The brokers will also be preparing most documents (for example, binders and mortgage qualifications) on their laptops, using forms prepared for them.

Mr. Banks has decided that at the current time, SBG cannot afford the $3000 per month charge for a direct T1 connection to the Internet. He has therefore decided to host his web site on the local ISP. The business will therefore retain its dial-up connection to the ISP for uploading files.

Mr. Banks would like his employees to share access to the Internet through the single modem. The same dial-up account used for accessing the ISP will therefore also be used for e-mail. Small-But-Growing Real Estate will register the domain name *smallbutgrowing.com* for its web site; employees will have e-mail addresses such as *employee@smallbutgrowing.com* that are accessible through the dial-up connection to the ISP.

The company's network will therefore consist of the following nodes:

- Nine workstations (one for each broker including Mr. Banks and one for each clerical assistant)
- One network printer
- One fax and e-mail server
- One network and file server

Because Mr. Banks wants to use a shared modem for Internet access, the network will require a router containing a modem. Although it is possible to have the router handle switching for the network, the network will perform better and be better suited to handle further growth if the configuration is broken into segments with their own hubs, which are then connected to the router.

You can find a network diagram in Figure 13-1. All connections are Fast Ethernet using Category 5 UTP wiring. For the most part, the real estate agents' workstations are connected to a single hub, which is on the same segment as the file server. This will maximize the brokers' access to forms and applications stored on the file server.

The clerical assistants' and Mr. Banks's workstations are part of the second segment, which contains the fax/e-mail server and the print

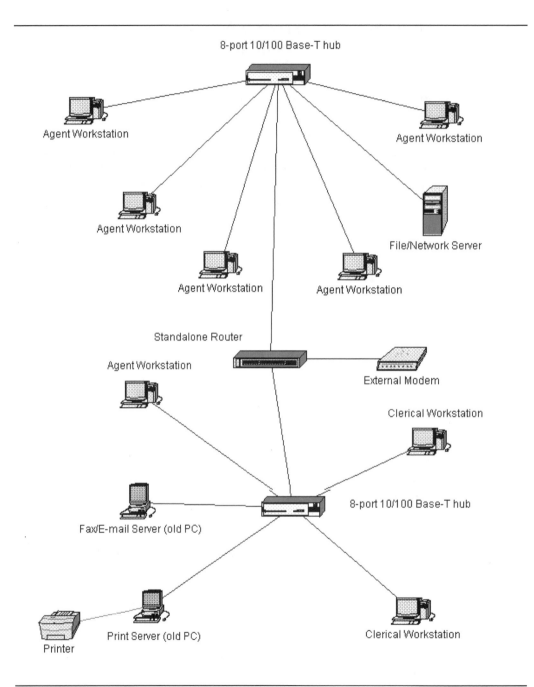

Figure 13-1:   **Network diagram for the Small-But-Growing Real Estate Company**

server. Two of the existing, older computers currently belonging to the company will be used to handle fax, e-mail, and print traffic.

The most expensive part of this network is the router. Although there are other solutions for shared Internet access (for example, the shared wireless modem discussed in Appendix A), the router is actually as cost effective as any other method. To keep costs down, the network uses two of the existing PCs as fax/e-mail and printer servers. The eight-port hubs are passive hubs; all routing is handled by the router. The file server has been placed on a different hub from the other two servers to help balance the traffic across the network.

In a small network such as this one, deciding where to put specific network devices is determined by two things: the physical location of the devices and the patterns of device usage. For example, most of the printing and faxing is done by clerical workers. Therefore, the printer server and fax server have been placed on the same network segment with the clerical workstations.

Although the clerical workers do need to load some applications from the file server, they place less of a load on it than the real estate agents. It therefore makes sense to place the file server on the same segment with most of the agent workstations.

Everyone uses e-mail. The choice to place it on the segment with the clerical workstations was made primarily because e-mail would be sharing a computer with faxing. (Real estate agencies do a great deal of faxing of contracts, binders, and mortgage application documentation.)

Can this network grow? Yes, it can grow quite easily. The eight-port hubs will support a few additional network devices each. If the company outgrows the hubs, then it can look at replacing them with either stackable hubs or switches. The company might also consider adding another network segment that connects directly to the router. Assuming that the new segment is as small as the existing two segments, then another eight-port hub would be sufficient and relatively low in cost. Given the nature of this business, it is unlikely that the company will outgrow the current router.

14

Ethernet Example 2: Medium Law Firm

Medium Law Firm (MLF) is a 55-year-old law firm that will be moving from offices on three floors of an old building into two floors of an office tower currently under construction several blocks away from its current location. MLF has been given the opportunity to wire its floors for telecommunications while construction is still in progress.

MLF has 30 attorneys (10 of whom are partners), 20 legal secretaries, six secretaries, one office manager, and one receptionist. Each partner has his or her own legal secretary; the remaining legal secretaries work for two attorneys each. The six secretaries perform tasks assigned to them by the office manager, who coordinates all the clerical work in the office.

In its current location, MLF has a thinnet Ethernet network that gives all clerical workers access to an e-mail server, a fax-server, and a file server. Some of the attorneys also have PCs in their offices that they use for e-mail.

The file server contains templates for commonly used legal forms. When a form is needed, a legal secretary loads a copy of the form from the server and fills it in as needed. The form is then printed and copied. All document copies are retained in filing cabinets.

MLF sees the move to new quarters as an opportunity to upgrade their network and data processing in general. First, they would like to move away from the slower thinnet Ethernet to at least Fast Ethernet, with the possibility of using Gigabit Ethernet for the network backbone (in other words, for the connection between floors). Second, they would like to move to permanent electronic storage of documents and the retrieval of those documents over the network. This will involve writing document copies on CD-Rs and providing one or more CD-ROM servers to make the documents available.

Third, MLF would like to consider a CD-ROM subscription to a law book service that could also be available over the network. In the long run, this would save the attorneys considerable money, given that MLF will need only one copy of each law book series, rather than relying on attorneys to purchase their own hard copies. Instead of purchasing multiple updates for multiple offices, all of the attorneys could share one networked copy. The idea is to eventually move to an all-electronic law library, including online access to legal search services such as Lexis from all offices rather than just from the library.

> Note: MLF understands that there may be some attorneys who purchase their own hard copy law books anyway, given that they like the "look" of all those books on their office shelves.

Finally, MLF is willing to invest in a T1 line so that the firm can have full-time access to the Internet. Internet connectivity will therefore be available through a router that also handles the connections between the two floors. (Should the firm ever choose to have a web site, the T1 line will also make it possible to do in-house hosting.)

There are actually two ways to begin designing a network of this type. One is from the "bottom up," where you start with the workstations and other end-user devices and then collect them into workgroups. You connect the workgroups with switches and then connect the entire network through some sort of backbone. Alternatively, you can work from the "top down," where you begin with the backbone, moving to workgroups in general and finally to the individual end-user devices.

Most successful information technology projects today are designed using a nominally top-down approach. In truth, you cannot design a network without considering the end-user devices as you specify backbones, routers, and switches. At the very least, you must have some idea of how many end-user devices (workstations and printers, for example) you will have and how they will interact with one another.

The Backbone and Wiring Closets

Because MLF is not occupying an entire building, it does not have the option of locating its main equipment room in the basement; the main equipment room must be somewhere on one of the two floors occupied by the law firm (the fourth and fifth floors of the building).

> *Note: In theory, MLF could negotiate with the building owners to allow them to place wiring in the basement. However, this presents a major security problem. The equipment room, the location where the T1 line to the ISP enters the building, is beyond the control of the firm's network administrators. In addition, there will be a long run of cable from the basement to the firm on the fourth and fifth floors.*

The reception desk, the office manager's office, and the secretarial pool are to be located on the fourth floor. The attorneys and the legal secretaries are distributed throughout both floors, resulting in more room on the fifth floor for computer equipment. Although there is a wiring closet on each floor, the fifth floor closet also contains the router that connects the entire network together.

As you can see in Figure 14-1, the backbone hardware is anchored by a router (the 3Com NETBuilder Chassis), which has four network modules: three Gigabit Ethernet modules and a module to connect the T1 line. Two of the Gigabit Ethernet modules are connected to multiprotocol switches, one for each floor. The switches connect the workgroups, which will be running Fast Ethernet, to the backbone. The third Gigabit Ethernet module connects the Gigabit Ethernet segment in the server room to the backbone.

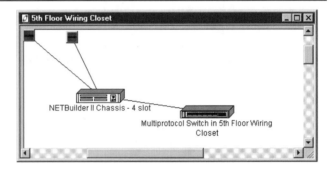

Figure 14-1:   Backbone hardware in the fifth floor wiring closet

Initially, the server room will contains four servers (a file/network server, an e-mail/fax server, and two CD-ROM servers) and a Gigabit Ethernet switch (see Figure 14-2). The switch is stackable, so that additional servers can be added as needed. Given the technology available at the time this book was written, this is the best possible use of Gigabit Ethernet: for a server farm and for a backbone.

You may question the use of Gigabit Ethernet with CD-ROM servers. CD-ROMs are considerably slower than any of the other storage devices on the network and at the current time cannot place data on the network fast enough to take full advantage of the bandwidth available with Gigabit Ethernet. However, this network is being designed with expansion in mind; as CD-ROM technology advances, the initial towers can be replaced with faster equipment. The fiber optic cabling for the Gigabit Ethernet will already be in place.

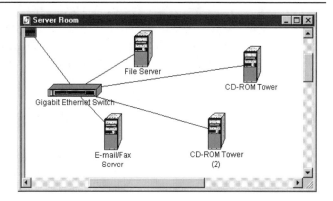

Figure 14-2:   The server room (fifth floor)

The fifth floor is a particularly good location for the router and the server room because the fifth floor is less heavily trafficked than the first floor, making the fifth floor easier to secure. In addition, all clients and maintenance personnel who go to the fifth floor will be accompanied by an MLF employee. All deliveries will be made to the fourth floor reception desk and carried by MLF employees to the fifth floor. (The six secretaries will share the escort and gofer duties.)

The fourth floor wiring closet contains just a switch to connect the workgroups on that floor (see Figure 14-3). It is connected to the router in the fifth floor wiring closet by fiber optic cabling. All workgroups on the fourth floor will be connected to this switch.

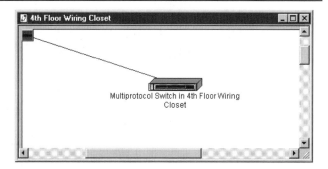

Figure 14-3:   The fourth floor wiring closet

Connecting End-User Devices

There are two basic strategies that MLF could use to connect its end-user devices to the network. It might create a collection of small network segments (for example, 8 to 16 devices) connected with a hub or switch. Each small segment would then be connected to the switch in the wiring closet. Alternatively, all workstations can be connected directly to the switches in the wiring closet. Assuming that the switch is a stackable switch, then the network can be expanded as needed.

As you might expect, there are benefits and drawbacks to both strategies.

   ◆ Using small network segments makes the network more fault tolerant. If the switch in the wiring closet goes down, each small network segment can continue to function independently.
   ◆ Using small network segments will be more expensive if the small segments use switches rather than passive hubs.
   ◆ Using small network segments will have better performance under heavy loads if most traffic is between the devices on a single subnet because there will be less traffic contending for the switches in the wiring closet and for the backbone. However, performance will suffer if a large portion of the traffic requires access to the servers or is between subnets.
   ◆ Using small network segments will make the network design more complex and problems therefore will be more difficult to troubleshoot. If passive hubs rather than switches are used for the subnets, troubleshooting will be extremely difficult because there will be no way to determine which device on a subnet has failed without physically checking each of the devices.
   ◆ Using only the switches in the wiring closets will provide more optimal routing (and thus better performance) because the switches will be able to route directly to end-user devices, rather than routing to other switches, which must then route within their own segment.

MLF decides to connect the workstations directly to a stackable switch on each floor. The switches will provide the simplest network layout, room for growth (although the most likely growth is to another floor in the same building), and good support for troubleshooting and maintenance.

For example, the wiring from the secretarial pool (six workstations and a networked printer) goes straight to the fourth floor closet (see Figure 14-4).

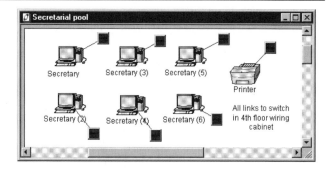

Figure 14-4: The fourth floor secretarial pool

Partners' offices (for example, Figure 14-5) and associates' offices (such as Figure 14-6) are also wired directly to the switch. However, the attorneys have made it clear that they want their own printers and that their legal secretaries should also have their own printers. Therefore, each workstation has its own direct-connect printer.

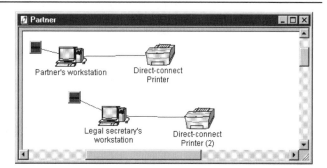

Figure 14-5: A partner's office

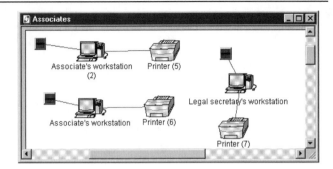

Figure 14-6:   An associate's office

> *Note: It is very true that many of the attorneys' printers will rarely be used. However, given that the cost of the printers and their maintenance is coming out of the partners' profits and therefore will not affect the company's overall budget, if the partners want their own printers, there is no reason not to install those printers.*

All end-user network devices use Fast Ethernet with UTP Category 5 wiring. Because the wiring will be running through a dropped ceiling and inside walls, plenum cabling will be used to adhere to local building codes. Given the rapidly decreasing price of Fast Ethernet hardware and the flexibility of UTP cabling, there is no real reason to use anything else within a single floor.

> *Note: Until UTP wiring is available to support Gigabit Ethernet and until the price comes down significantly, it will still be too costly to use Gigabit Ethernet to connect end-user devices to an Ethernet network.*

15

Ethernet Example 3: Large Insurance Company

The Large Insurance Company (LIC) is a 125-year-old business with headquarters located in a major East Coast city. Like many insurance companies, LIC has used computers to process premiums and claims since the 1960s. At this time, the company is in the midst a major upgrade of its computing systems that was triggered by its need to make its software year 2000 compliant.

Currently, LIC has a number of host-based programs running on a mainframe. The programs are written in COBOL and accessed by a variety of terminals connected to the mainframe. Some users work with older dumb terminals, while other users have PCs that perform terminal emulation. Thick coax cabling runs vertically through the entire 10-floor headquarters building. Connections to the thick coax backbone are made with thin coax running in the walls and, in some cases, under carpets.

LIC has decided to move to a client-server processing system, replacing all of its terminals with PCs and using the mainframe as a file server. Several smaller departmental servers will be added as well. A major software-development effort will be replacing the majority of the legacy code with new database-driven client-server applications.

As a result, LIC has made a commitment to rewiring the building, installing a fiber optic backbone and using Category 5 UTP wiring within floors. The new cabling will be run through walls and drop ceilings; there will be no more cabling under carpets.

The Machine Room

LIC's mainframe is located on the third floor of the building in an environmentally controlled, glass-walled enclosure with a raised floor (the proverbial "glass house"). Rather than move the mainframe, the new network will have its main hardware connections added to the current machine room.

Connecting a mainframe to an Ethernet is somewhat different than connecting desktop devices. The typical mainframe uses specialized processors known as *I/O channels* to off-load I/O processing from the mainframe's processors. The router through which the mainframe is connected must therefore include a module that can connect to an I/O channel.

An off-the-shelf router does not contain this type of connectivity. ILC must therefore purchase a router chassis to which a "channel interface processor" with at least one parallel channel module can be added. ILC chooses a five-slot router (the Cisco 7000 in Figure 15-1), adding one module for the mainframe and four modules that each provide two Gigabit Ethernet fiber optic connections. As you can see in Figure 15-2, the connection between the mainframe and

the router is indeed made through the I/O channel's parallel interface. The Gigabit Ethernet ports can then be used to connect switches on each of the individual floors into a backbone network.

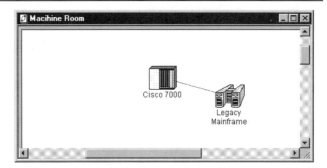

Figure 15-1:   Connecting a mainframe directly to a router

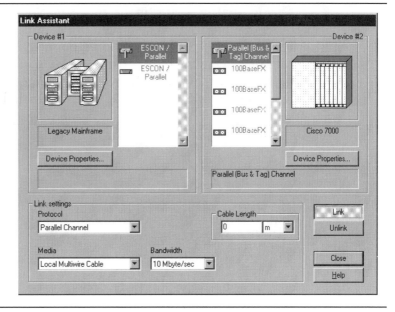

Figure 15-2:   The link between the mainframe and the router

In addition to the router and the mainframe, the machine room contains a number of system terminals (those used to manage the mainframe), a high-speed laser printer used for high-volume output, and

the switch for network devices on the third floor. This switch is a multispeed, stackable switch similar to those used for the law firm discussed in Chapter 14. It has a Gigabit Ethernet port to connect to the router and a number of Fast Ethernet ports for connecting network devices.

Departmental Subnets

Although LIC's mainframe can handle an enormous amount of processing, the LIC IT staff have recognized that the size of the company means that the mainframe is best used by dedicating it to processing premiums and claims, off-loading corporate administrative tasks to departmental servers.

The accounting department, for example, handles all accounting tasks that are unrelated to premiums and claims, such as payroll, travel, supplies, utilities, building maintenance, and so on. The accounting department uses a client-server accounting package running on their own server, which is connected to the accounting workstations with a stackable switch (see Figure 15-3).

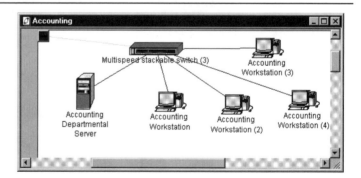

Figure 15-3:   The accounting department subnet

In Chapter 14, you read that subnets can make a network harder to administer and troubleshoot, and may even slow down performance. However, the situation with LIC is somewhat different from that of the law firm. The departments with their own subnets perform most of their work off their own servers; other departments rarely, if ever, have need to access those servers; and the departmental workstations rarely need data stored elsewhere. The workstations on the subnet will therefore perform much better if their traffic stays on a local subnet, rather than traveling all the way to a floor-wide switch. Given that the accounting department uses data stored on the mainframe infrequently, slower performance reaching that data is acceptable.

All devices on a departmental subnet are equipped with Fast Ethernet hardware and are connected to the departmental subnet switch with Category 5 UTP plenum wiring. The departmental switch then connects to the switch in the floor's wiring cabinet using fiber optic cabling and a Gigabit Ethernet interface.

Other departmental subnets include human relations, training (in-house training for salespeople), IT, building maintenance, clerical services, and administration (including the CEO's and vice president's offices).

Connecting Premium Processing, Claims Processing, and Customer Service

At any given time, there are between 500 and 600 people working in the LIC building handling premium and claims processing. In addition, there are just over 300 customer service specialists who interact with customers over the telephone. Both of these groups of employees need access to data stored on the mainframe. The question facing network designers is therefore how to connect such a large group of users to an Ethernet.

Premium and Claims Processing

The new software designed for this premium and claims processing uses a hybrid object/relational database residing on the mainframe. The applications to manipulate that database run on the end-user workstations. However, the employees performing these tasks do not need real-time access to the mainframe; their function is primarily data entry. They can therefore store data on the hard disks of their workstations and then upload all the data to the mainframe as a batch.

Given that access to the mainframe, and therefore to the backbone, is sporadic, the premium and claims processing workstations can be grouped into a hierarchy of subnets, reducing the number of connections to the backbone ultimately to one, as in the small example in Figure 15-4. Although this illustration shows workgroups of four connected to a hub, in reality the workgroups will need to be somewhat larger.

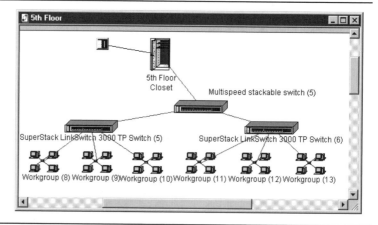

Figure 15-4:   A small example of a workstation and switch hierarchy

Why? Because the hierarchy of workstations and switches should be configured so that it does not exceed the limit of seven switches to reach the backbone. As you may remember from Chapter 5, this is the maximum number of switches in a row that provide acceptable performance. Keep in mind that there is another switch in the wiring closet and that there is a hub connecting each workgroup, allowing a maximum of five switches between any workstation and the backbone.

Do personnel who are engaged primarily in data entry need complete PCs as workstations? In this case, probably not. A thin client —a machine with a CPU, main memory, and hard drive but no removable storage—is probably a good choice for such users. A thin client machine can load a clean copy of its operating system off a server (in this case, the mainframe) each morning when the machine is booted. This arrangement provides several advantages:

- There is no way for an employee to take confidential information away with him or her because the machines have no removable storage.
- The machines are less susceptible to problems because users cannot load any of their own software onto the machines. (This assumes that the machines are not connected to the Internet, which is the case here.)
- If software problems do occur, the machine can easily be reloaded with a fresh, clean copy of its operating system and software.

Customer Service

The customer service specialists are another story altogether. Unlike the data entry personnel, whose database access is easily predicted, customer service queries are ad hoc. In other words, there is no way to predict what queries the specialists will be performing; the queries arise at the spur of the moment (whenever a customer calls in) and may never arise again. The customer service specialists must therefore have real-time access to the database on the mainframe. The speed with which they receive responses to their queries will certainly affect customer satisfaction.

> Note; Relational databases excel at processing ad hoc queries, which makes one ideal for LIC. Prior to this major system upgrade, many questions received by the customer service specialists could not be answered while the customer was on the

telephone. Answers had to be researched manually and then a return phone call placed to the customer. The new software will therefore provide significantly enhanced customer service.

The customer service specialists must therefore be connected as close to the backbone as possible. In other words, we want to reduce the number of switches through which a packet must travel before reaching a workstation and/or the mainframe.

The LIC network designers therefore use stackable switches that are connected directly to the switch in the wiring closet. Each workstation therefore sends packets only through its workgroup switch and the switch in the wiring closet before reaching the backbone, as in Figure 15-5.

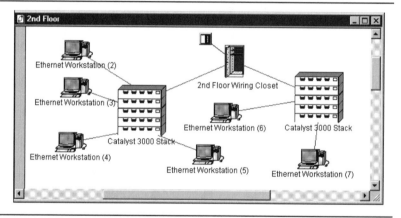

Figure 15-5:   Subnetting for real-time backbone access

As you look at Figure 15-5, keep in mind that the switch in the wiring closet is also stackable. Therefore, if each workgroup switch stack can handle 50 workstations, then 12 such stacks will be needed to handle the 300 customer service representatives.

Why not use routers in this situation rather than switches? Performance is certainly a major issue and routers can optimize routes whereas switches cannot. In making the decision to go with the less expensive switches, the designers looked at the customer service representatives' data traffic patterns. The representatives rarely communicate with one another. Instead, almost all of their data communications is with the mainframe. Therefore, the routing is very simple: from the workstation, to the workgroup switch, to the backbone switch, to the router in the machine room, to the mainframe. There is no more efficient or possible routing. Therefore, LIC would gain little in this case by using routers rather than switches.

A

Home Networking

Throughout this book, you have been reading about Ethernets for business use. Networks are, however, making their way into our homes as well. Many families have multiple computers in several locations throughout a house. A home network lets these computers share files, a common printer, and perhaps a modem. (A home network also enables multiplayer gaming....)

You can certainly use any of the techniques discussed in the body of this book for a home network. (For example, the author of this book has a wired 10BASE-T network using an eight-port hub and Category 5 UTP cabling.) However, there are two emerging solutions that are designed specifically for home use, one wired and one wireless.

Home Networking Using Existing Home Wiring

Most of today's new homes are wired with Category 3 UTP cabling, although other types of wiring are found in older homes. The Home Phoneline Networking Alliance (HomePNA)—a group of commercial organizations (including 3Com, AMD, AT&T, Compaq, Epigram, Hewlett-Packard, IBM, Intel, Lucent Technologies, Rockwell Semiconductor Systems, and Tut Systems)—has been formed to promote a standard for the creation of networks using that existing wiring, whatever it may be. The group's goal is to bring compatible products from a variety of vendors to market as quickly as possible. The first hardware designed for consumer purchase appeared on the market in early 1999.

The initial technology adopted by HomePNA, known as Home-Run, was developed by Tut Systems. It provides 1 Mbs transmission over standard telephone wiring. Data transmissions can share the same wiring as POTS services because the HomeRun transmissions use a higher frequency than voice transmissions. This means that a HomeRun network can be installed in a home where all existing phone lines are in use without requiring additional wiring.

> *Note: HomeRun is not 10BASE-T, although its hardware can be connected to a device through a 10BASE-T port.*

HomeRun technology does not require a hub, router, splitter, filter, or network terminator. It is designed to work over the often rather random layout of telephone cabling in a home. The two products licensed by Tut Systems to other vendors for retail sale include an adapter for devices already equipped with 10BASE-T hardware and a NIC for those that are not. (NIC drivers are available only for Windows 95, Windows 98, and Windows NT.) The adapter is platform-independent: It works with *any* platform that has Ethernet capabilities, through either a NIC or Ethernet hardware on the motherboard.

> *Note: HomePNA hopes that eventually HomeRun technology will be built into computers, printers, and modems so that all an*

*end user will need to do to network a piece of equipment is plug
it into a telephone jack.*

The devices in a HomeRun network can be up to 500 feet apart, providing support for a home of up to 10,000 square feet. The initial standard supports up to 25 devices (computers, printers, modems, and so on).

HomeRun networking is designed for the peer-to-peer networking supported by operating systems such as Windows 95, Windows 98, and the Macintosh OS. Because it has no inherent routing capabilities, to support stand-alone servers you must connect those servers to a HomeRun adapter using standard 10BASE-T. The adapter then functions as a hub.

The HomePNA solution to home networking has several advantages:

♦ It is relatively inexpensive (no more than $100 per network device).
♦ It is easy to install.
♦ It requires no new wiring and can use any existing telephone jacks.
♦ It can share wiring with voice telephone service and does not interfere with the quality of voice transmissions.
♦ It supports printer, modem, and file sharing through an operating system's peer-to-peer networking facilities. Multiple users can share a single ISP connection.

There is one potential security hole in using telephone wiring for network transmissions: If the wiring travels outside the home and to the telephone pole at any point, that signal can be intercepted. One acceptable solution to the problem would be to encrypt data when it leaves the premises so that it will be unintelligible to any unauthorized person reading it.

Wireless Home Networking

The wireless solution—Symphony from Proxim—uses radio frequency transmissions to enable computers to communicate with one another. It has a maximum data transfer rate of 1.6 Mbps.

There are four hardware pieces to the system:

- An ISA card for Intel-based desktop computers containing a radio transceiver (Figure A-1)

Figure A-1:   The Symphony ISA card

- A PC card for Intel-based laptop computers containing a radio transceiver (Figure A-2)

Figure A-2:   The Symphony PC card

♦ A bridge with a radio transceiver that can be used with a Macintosh or to connected wired services such as a cable modem or ISDN to the wireless network (Figure A-3)

Figure A-3:   The Symphony wireless bridge

♦ A wireless 56K modem that is accessible from any computer with a Symphony transceiver (Figure A-4)

Because the bridge and modem are wireless, they can be placed anywhere in the house and do not need to necessarily be next to the computers that are using them. The exception to this is when you are using a bridge to connect a Macintosh to the network; in that case, the bridge must be connected to the Macintosh with a 10BASE-T cable.

Symphony's components have a maximum range of approximately 150 feet, although the materials used in construction of the home will have some effect. For example, radio signals do not travel as well through cinder block as they do through wood. A Symphony network is also limited to a maximum of 10 computers.

Symphony is designed for peer-to-peer networking, although there is certainly no reason that it cannot integrate with a dedicated file

Figure A-4: The Symphony wireless modem

server. However, the intention of the home networking design is that computers typically connect only to exchange files and that most sharing involves a modem and/or printer.

There are several benefits to using a wireless solution in the home.

♦ Installation is easy (plug-and-play).
♦ The wireless modem allows multiple users to use the same ISP connection at the same time, requiring only one phone line for all household members. (The exception to this is America Online, which does not support the sharing of the single connection between multiple computers.)
♦ There is no need to worry about the suitability of wiring already in the home for networking.
♦ Components connected to the network are mobile. For example, you can move a laptop with a PC card to any location in the house, and perhaps the yard, and still have access to the network.

♦ You can probably afford to purchase a better printer because all you will need is one that can be shared by all users.

B

Vendor List

The body of this book mentions many specific products as examples of Ethernet concepts. This appendix contains contact information for the manufacturers of those products. Web addresses were correct at the time this book was written.

A mention of a product in this book does not constitute an endorsement of that product. It is up to you to evaluate products yourself to determine which best meet your particular needs.

Allied Telesyn
Transceivers, switches, hubs
19015 North Creek Parkway, #200
Bothell, WA 98011
Voice: (800) 424-4284
Fax: (425) 489-9191
Web site: http://www.alliedtelesyn.com

Apple Computer
AppleTalk, AppleShare, Macintosh OS
1 Infinite Loop
Cupertino, CA 95014
Voice: (408) 996-1010
Web site: http://www.apple.com

Banyan
VINES network operating system
120 Flanders Road
P.O. box 5013
Westboro, MA 01581
Voice: (800) 2-BANYAN
Fax: (508) 898-1755
Web site: http://www.banyan.com

Belden Wire & Cable Company
Network cabling
2200 U.S. Highway 27 South
P.O. Box 1980
Richmond, IN 47374
Voice: (765) 983-5200
Fax: (765) 983-5294
Web site: http://www.belden.com

Belkin Components
Network cabling
501 West Walnut Street
Compton, CA 90220
Voice: (800) 2-BELKIN
Fax: (310) 898-1111
Web site: http://www.belkin.com

Caldera, Inc.
Network-ready operating system (Linux)
240 West Center Street
Orem, Utah 84057
Voice: (801) 765-4999
Fax: (801) 765-1313
Web site: http://www.calderasystems.com

Citrix Systems
MetaFrame
6400 Northwest 6th Way
Ft. Lauderdale, FL 33309
Voice: (954) 267-3000
Fax: (954) 267-9319
Web site: http://www.citrix.com

Farallon Communications, Inc.
Daisy-chainable Ethernet adapters (EtherWave), PCMCIA network
adapters
3089 Teagarden Street
San Leandro, CA 94577
Voice: (510) 814-5000
Fax: (510) 814-5015
Web site: http://www.farallon.com

Hewlett-Packard
Hubs, switches, hub and switch management software
(NetCenter), hardware print servers
3000 Hanover Street
Palo Alto, CA 94304
Voice: (650) 857-1501
Fax: (650) 857-5518
Web site: http://www.hp.com

HomePNA (Home Phoneline Network Alliance)
Standards for home networking using standard telephone wiring
Web site: http://www.homepna.org

IBM
Network operating system (OS/2 Lan Server)
1133 Westchester Avenue
White Plains, NY 10604
Voice: (800) IBM 4YOU
Fax: (770) 863-3030
Web site: http://www.ibm.com

Infinite Technologies
I-Queue Server for Windows 95
11433 Cronridge Drive
Owings Mills, MD 21117
Voice: (800) 678-1097
Fax: (410) 363-3779
Web site: http://www.ihub.com

MangoSoft Corporation
Virtual server software (Medley98)
1500 West Park Drive
Suite 190
Westborough, MA 01581
Voice: (888) 88-MANGO
Fax: (508) 898-9166
Web site: http://www.mangosoft.com

Meridian Data, Inc.
Headless network file server (Snap! Server)
5615 Scotts Valley Drive
Scotts Valley, CA 95066
Voice: (831) 438-3100
Fax: (831) 438-6816
Web site: http://www.meridian-data.com

Microsoft Corporation
Network operating systems (Microsoft Windows LAN Manager,
Windows NT, Windows 2000), Windows OS
One Microsoft Way
Redmond, WA 98052
Voice: (425) 882-8090
Web site: http://www.microsoft.com

Miramar Systems, Inc.
Multiplatform network integration software (PC MACLAN)
10 East Yananoli Street
Santa Barbara, CA 93101
Voice: (800) 862-2526
Fax: (805) 965-1824
Web site: http://www.miramarsys.com

Neon Software
Network mapping software (LANsurveyor), multiprotocol
network analyzer (TrafficWatch, now integrated into NetMinder
Ethernet)
3685 Mt. Diablo Boulevard
Suite 253
Lafayette, CA 94549
Voice: (800) 334-NEON
Fax: (925) 283-6507
Web site: http://www.neon.com

NetCracker Technology Company
Network design and simulation software (NetCracker Designer,
NetCracker Professional)
1159 Main Street
Waltham, MA 02154
Voice: (800) 477-5785
Fax: (781) 736-1735
Web site: http://www.netcracker.com

Netopia, Inc.
Multiplatform network integration software (Timbuktu Pro),
routers
2470 Mariner Square Loop
Alameda, CA 94501
Voice: (510) 814-5000
Fax: (510) 814-5025
Web site: http://www.netopia.com

Novell Corporation
Network operating system (Novell NetWare)
2211 North First Street
San Jose, CA 95131
Voice: (408) 968-5000
Web site: http://www.novell.com

Optical Access International
CD-ROM servers (Maxtet/CD Enterprise)
*Contact is through regional representatives. To find the one nearest you,
see* http://www2.oai.com/CONTACT/contact.html
Web site: http://www.oai.com

Proxim, Inc.
Wireless network hardware (RangeLAN2, Symphony)
295 North Bernardo Avenue
Mountain View, CA 94043
Voice: (800) 229-1630
Fax: (650) 960-1984
Web site: http://www.proxim.com

Red Hat Software, Inc.
Network-ready operating system (Linux)
P.O. Box 13588
Research Triangle Park, NC 27709
Voice: (800) 454-5502
Fax: (919) 547-0024
Web site: http://www.redhat.com

A. T. Schneider Communications, Inc.
Wireless network hardware (FiRLAN)
101-21 Antares Drive
Ottawa, Ontario K2E 7T8
CANADA
Voice: (613) 723-1103
Fax: (613) 723-6895
Web site: http://www.firlan.com

The Siemon Company
Network cabling
Siemon Business Park
76 Westbury Park Road
Watertown, CT 06795
Voice: (860)274-2523
Fax: (860) 945-4225
Web site: http://www.siemon.com

3Com Corporation
NICs, hubs, and switches
5400 Bayfront Plaza
Santa Clara, CA 95052
Voice: (800) NET-3COM
Fax: (408) 326-5001
Web site: http://www.3com.com

Thursby Software Systems, Inc.
Multiplatform network integration software (DAVE)
5840 West Interstate 20, Suite 100
Arlington, TX 78017
Voice: (817) 478-5070
Fax: (817) 561-2313
Web site: http://www.thursby.com

Triticom
Network monitoring software (LANdecoder)
9971 Valley View Road
Eden Prairie, MN 55344
Voice: (612) 937-0772
Web site: http://www.triticom.com

University of Melbourne
Columbia AppleTalk Package (CAP)
Web site: http://www.cs.mu.oz.au/appletalk/cap.html

University of Michigan
netatalk
Web site: http://www.umich.edu/~rsug/netatalk/

Xircom
Network adapters (RealPort)
2300 Corporate Center Drive
Thousand Oaks, CA 91320
Voice: (805) 376-9300
Fax: (805) 376-9311
Web site: http://www.xircom.com

Glossary

AAUI (Apple Attachment Unit Interface): A generic port on an Apple Macintosh or Macintosh-compatible network device to which a specific Ethernet transceiver is connected.

Acknowledged connectionless exchange: A data communications exchange in which each packet is routed by the most efficient pathway. The receiver lets the sender know when each packet has been received.

AppleShare: An add-on to the Macintosh Operating System that permits the sharing of files from a centralized location.

AppleTalk: A set of protocols designed primarily for use by Macintosh computers. However, AppleTalk protocols are also available for Windows 95, Windows NT, and Linux.

Application server: A file server that contains applications for network users to fun.

Attenuation: Loss of signal strength due to friction on the surface of the wire.

AUI (Attachment Unit Interface): A generic port on a network device to which a specific Ethernet transceiver is connected.

Auto-negotiation: A process during which a hub and a NIC exchange information about the highest speed each can handle to determine the speed at which transmission will take place.

Backbone: A network to which only other networks are connected.

Bandwidth: The number of bits that can travel together at the same time on a single transmission medium.

Baseband: A transmission medium that can carry only one signal at a time.

BNC (barrel) connector: The type of connector used to attached devices to a thinnet network.

Bridge: In theory, a device that connects two network segments and can route transmissions to the correct segment; in practice, a switch.

Broadband: A transmission medium that can carry multiple signals at one time.

Bus topology: The fundamental topology of an Ethernet network segment, in which all devices are connected to a single transmission medium with unconnected ends.

Carrier: A signal on an Ethernet transmission medium indicating that a frame/packet is currently on the network and that another frame cannot be transmitted at that time.

Category 3, 4, and 5: Grades of UTP cabling. The higher the grade, the more often the wire is twisted.

CD-ROM jukebox: Specialized hardware that can choose one of many CD-ROMs to make available to a user.

CD-ROM servers: Specialized hardware that can simultaneously make multiple CD-ROMs available to multiple users.

Coaxial cable: Network cabling made up of a central copper wire, layers of shielding, and a copper mesh.

Collision: The event that occurs when two devices on a network attempt to transmit frames at exactly the same time.

Collision domain: A section of a network, comprising a single Ethernet bus , to which devices attached to that bus compete for access; a more precise term for an Ethernet network segment.

Connection-oriented exchange: A data communications conversation that assumes that there is a virtual circuit between a sender and a receiver and that every packet that is part of a single message travels through the circuit.

CRC (cyclical redundancy check): The last field of an Ethernet packet, used for error checking.

Crossover cable: A cable in which the input and output wires are reversed at one end.

Crossover port: A port on a hub for use in daisy chaining with another hub. The input and output wires are reversed so that the two hubs do not send and receive on the same wires.

Crosstalk: The bleeding of signals from one pair of wires in a cable to another.

CSMA/CA (Carrier Sense Multiple Access with Collision Avoidance): The MAC protocol used by many wireless transmission devices. Unlike CSMA/CD, this protocol does not detect collisions.

CSMA/CD (Carrier Sense Multiple Access with Collision Detection): The MAC used by Ethernet. Devices detect the presence of a frame on the network by listening for a carrier signal. If none is present, a frame can be transmitted. Devices also detect collisions and repeat colliding transmissions after a random wait interval.

Daisy-chain topology: An Ethernet topology in which the bus is formed by independent lengths of media passing through each network device.

Data field: The portion of an Ethernet packet containing meaninful data.

Database server: A file server that runs a database management system and provides data management capabilities to a user.

Datagram: The TCP/IP term for a network packet.

DBMS (database management system): Software that interacts with stored data to store and retrieve data based on commands issued by a user or application program.

Destination address: The physical address of a network device that is to receive an Ethernet packet.

Drop cable: A single, unbroken stretch of thick coaxial cable into which transceivers tab by cutting through the cable shielding to make physical contact with the copper mesh layer and central copper wire.

DTE (data terminal equipment): Any device that will be connected to a network.

E-mail server: A computer dedicated to the sending and receiving of e-mail.

Ethernet: A standard describing the way in which computers on a network gain access to the network media.

Fast Ethernet: Ethernet that transfers data at a maximum of 100 megabits per second.

Fax server: A computer connected to a modem that dials out to send faxes and answers incoming fax calls.

FCS (frame check sequence): The last field of an Ethernet packet, used for error checking.

File server: A repository for files that are to be shared over a network.

Frame: A package of data and control information that travels as a unit across the network; also known as a *packet*.

Frequency hopping: A security technique used by wireless networking hardware, whereby the transmission frequency varies continuously.

Frozen yellow garden hose: The nickname given to thick coaxial cable, based on its yellow outer coating and inability to bend easily.

FTP (file transfer protocol): The TCP/IP protocol that supports file transfer over a network.

Full-duplex: Transmissions in two directions at the same time.

Gigabit Ethernet: Ethernet that transfers data at a maximum of 1000 megabits (1 gigabit) per second.

Half-duplex: Transmission in only one direction at a time.

HTTP (hypertext transfer protocol): The TCP/IP protocol that supports the transfer of hypertext documents.

Hub: A network device that contains the wiring for a bus.

Internet: When written in all lowercase letters (*internet*), a WAN that connects multiple LANs into a larger network. When written with a leading uppercase letter (*Internet*), the global network that supports the World Wide Web.

Intranet: A LAN that includes a World Wide Web server.

I/O channel: A special processor used in a mainframe to handle input and output operations.

IEEE (Institute of Electrical and Electronic Engineers): The organization whose LAN standards committee prepares Ethernet standards for adoption and potential adoption.

IP (internet protocol): The TCP/IP protocol that provides connectionless service along with logical network addressing, packet switching, and dynamic routing.

IPX (internet packet exchange): The IPX/SPX protocol that performs translations between physical addressing from layers below to logical addressing for layers above and connectionless routing functions.

IPX/SPX: Protocols developed for Novell NetWare, a network operating system, based on prior work by Xerox at its PARC (Palo Alto Research Center) facility.

ISO (International Standards Organization): The international body that approves technology standards.

LAN (local area network): A network confined to a small geographic area—such as a floor, a single building, or a group of buildings in close physical proximity (for example, a college campus or an office park)—that is almost always owned by a single organization.

Length field: In an Ethernet data packet, the number of meaningful types of data; in an Ethernet management packet, the type of management information present in the frame.

LocalTalk: Apple Computer's proprietary cabling that can be used with the AppleTalk network protocols.

Linux: An open-source, free implementation of UNIX used extensively for hosting web sites.

MAC (media access control) address: A unique address assigned to a piece of hardware on a network. MAC addresses must be unique throughout the entire network.

MAC (media access control): A method for managing the access of multiple devices to a single, shared network medium.

MAN (metropolitan area network): An outdated term describing a network that covers an entire city. Today, the concept of a MAN has largely been replaced by the WAN.

Managed hubs: Hubs that can capture statistics about network traffic and accept control commands from a workstation on the network.

MAU (medium attachment unit): The hardware used to connect a network device to a hub, switch, bridge, router, or gateway in a star topology.

MDI (medium dependent interface): The cable that connects a Fast Ethernet transceiver to the network medium.

Metcalfe, Robert: The inventor of Ethernet.

Microsoft Windows LAN Manager: A network operating system that is part of Windows for Workgroups, Windows 95, Windows 98, and Windows NT.

MII (media-independent interface): A device used with Fast Ethernet between an external transceiver and a NIC.

Mirror: A copy of a web server to which traffic can be routed to balance the load on the primary web server.

Multicast address: An address that is recognized by a group of devices on a network.

Multimode cabling: Fiber optic cabling that reflects light at more than one angle.

Multispeed hub: A hub that can handle more than one transmission speed, typically 10 Mbs and 100 Mbs.

NetBEUI (network BIOS extended user interface): Protocols used by Windows 95, Windows 98, and Windows NT.

NetPC: A stand-alone PC with a hard drive but no floppy or CD-ROM drives.

Network: A combination of hardware and software that allows computers and other peripherals (for example, printers and modems) to communicate with one another through some form of telecommunications media (for example, telephone lines).

Network computer: A computer with a Java Virtual Machine and a World Wide Web browser. It has its own CPU and can process data retrieved from a server.

Network discovery: The process of using software to determine the devices on a network and the layout of that network.

Network management: In terms of software, software that can monitor network traffic and report on network performance; in the fullest sense, a group of tasks that includes the maintenance and upgrading of a functioning network.

Network segment: A section of network transmission medium to which devices attached to that medium compete for access.

NFS (network file system): The TCP/IP protocol that supports file sharing between networks.

NIC (network interface card): An expansion board that contains the hardware necessary for a piece of hardware to communicate with a network. NIC hardware may also be built onto a motherboard.

Node: Each distinct piece of hardware on a network.

Noise: Any unwanted signal on network transmission media.

NOS (network operating system): Software that manages the transfer of data throughout the network.

Novell NetWare: A network operating system.

100BASE-FX: The Gigabit Ethernet standard for 1000 Mbps transmission over fiber optic cable.

100BASE-TX: The Fast Ethernet standard that supports 100 Mbps transmission over Category 5 UTP wiring.

1000BASE-T: The Ethernet standard that supports 1000 Mbps transmission over Category 5 UTP wiring.

OS/2 LAN Server: A network-ready operating system that can work with TCP/IP, IPX/SPX, or NetBEUI.

OSI (Open System interconnect) Reference Model: A world-wide standard protocol that provides the underlying theory for actual protocol implementations.

Packet: A package of data and control information that travels as a unit across the network; also known as a *frame*.

Passive hub: A hub that accepts an incoming signal, amplifies it, and broadcasts it to all devices on the network.

Patch cable: A relatively short cable that connects a network device to a wall outlet or directly to a hub or wiring closet.

PHY (Physical Layer device): A Fast Ethernet transceiver.

Physical layer: The bottom layer of a protocol stack that refers to the network hardware.

Plenum cabling: Cabling that has a plastic coating that is less toxic when burned than standard cabling. Plenum cabling is required for installation is spaces through which breathable air passes.

Port: A connector on a network device used to connect the device to the network.

POTS (plain old telephone service): Standard voice-grade telephone service.

Preamble: The first portion of an Ethernet packet that is used to synchronize the transmission.

Print queue: A list of jobs waiting to be printed.

Print server: Hardware, software, or a combination of both that manage a shared network printer.

Propagation delay: The time it takes for a signal to be broadcast and read by all devices on a network.

Protocol: A specification of how a computer will format and transfer data.

Protocol stack: A group of layered protocols that work together to effect network data transfers.

Remote control: Controlling the action of another computer over a network.

Repeater: A piece of hardware that amplifies and retransmits a network signal. Repeater functionality is built into hubs, switches, bridges, and routers.

RJ-11: The connector used with UTP wiring for standard telephone connections.

RJ-45: The connector used with UTP wiring for Ethernet.

Router: A device for connecting network segments that can optimize the path along which packets travel.

Server farm: A group of file servers all on the same network file segment, usually connected by fiber optic cabling.

Single mode cabling: Fiber optic cabling that reflects light at only one angle.

SMTP (simple mail transfer protocol): The TCP/IP protocol that supports the transfer of e-mail.

SNMP (simple network management protocol): The TCP/IP protocol that provides basic functions for managing network devices.

Source address: The hardware address of the network device sending an Ethernet packet.

Spanning-tree algorithm: Software within a switch that ensures there is only one path in a network from one switch to another, avoiding looping problems.

Spooling: Saving print jobs on a disk where they will wait until a printer is free to print them.

SPX (sequenced packet exchange): The IPX/SPX protocol that provides connection-oriented service between the addresses identified by IPX.

Stackable hubs: Hubs that can be connected so that they appear to be a single, large hub to the network.

Standard Ethernet: Ethernet that transfers data at a maximum of 10 megabits per second.

Star topology: A network topology in which all devices are connected to a single central device.

Start frame delimiter: The last eight bits of the Ethernet packet preamble that mark the preamble and the start of the information-bearing parts of the frame.

Structured cabling system: The design of the wiring of commercial buildings for data and telecommunications.

Switch: A device used to connect multiple network segments or devices. Switches can perform routing to the correct network segment rather than broadcasting transmissions to the entire network as hubs do.

TCP (transmission control protocol): A TCP/IP protocol that provides connection-oriented service, including error correction and flow control.

TCP/IP (Transmission Control Protocol/Internet Protocol): The protocols used by the Internet.

Telnet: The TCP/IP protocol that supports remote terminal sessions.

Terminator: A connector at each end of a thinnet network that prevents the unwanted reflection of signals from the ends of the bus back down the network medium.

10BASE5: The Ethernet standard that supports 100 Mbps transmission over thick coaxial cabling.

10BASE-T: The Ethernet standard that supports 10 Mbps transmission over UTP cabling.

10BASE2: The Ethernet standard that supports 10 Mbps transmission over thin coaxial cabling.

Thicknet: An Ethernet network using thick coaxial cabling (10BASE5).

Thin client: A network device that has a CPU and therefore may be able to process data locally. It may or may not have a hard drive, but does not have a floppy or CD-ROM drive. A thin client loads all its software over the network from a file server and processes the data locally (10BASE2).

Thinnet: An Ethernet network using thin coaxial cabling.

Throughput: The number of bits that arrive at a destination per unit time.

Topology: The physical layout of network devices and the transmission media that connect them.

Transceiver: A piece of hardware that sits between a network device and the network medium, ensuring that the device receives the correct type of signal, regardless of the type of medium in use. Today, transceiver hardware is often built into NICs or on motherboards.

Transceiver cable: A cable that connects a transceiver to a NIC.

UDP (user datagram protocol): A TCP/IP protocol that provides connectionless service.

Unacknowledged connectional exchange: A data communications exchange in which each packet is routed by the most efficient pathway. The receiver does not let the sender know when each packet has been received.

UNIX: An operating system that includes network operating system capabilities.

Unmanaged hub: A hub that accepts an incoming signal, amplifies it, and broadcasts it to all devices on the network.

UTP (unshielded twisted pair wiring): Network cable containing one or more pairs of copper wires that are twisted in a spiral manner.

Vampire clamp: A 10BASE5 (thicknet) transceiver that cuts through the coaxial cable to make physical contact with the copper mesh and wiring inside.

Virtual circuit: A single identified transmission path between a sender and a receiver, made up of a collection of transmission media and hardware that connects network segments. A virtual circuit remains in place for the duration of a single conversation.

Virtual server: A file server that appears as a single hard drive to users but is made up of a portion of the hard drives of more than one computer.

WAN (wide area network): A network that covers a large geographic area, such as a city, a state, or one or more countries.

Web server: A file server that is hosting a World Wide Web site.

Windows-based terminal: A device with no local processing power. It is designed to access Windows programs stored and executed on a server through the Windows Terminal Server program.

Wiring closet: A locked cabinet that contains the wiring for an Ethernet bus.

Index